UNITED NATIONS CONFERENCE ON TRADE AND DEVELOPMENT

Social Science Library
Oxford University Library Services
Manor Road
Oxford OX1 3UQ

WITHDRAWN

T
177
.044
.GLO

GLOBALIZATION OF R&D AND DEVELOPING COUNTRIES

Proceedings of the Expert Meeting
Geneva
24-26 January 2005

UNITED NATIONS
New York and Geneva, 2005

NOTE

As the focal point in the United Nations system for investment and technology, and building on 30 years of experience in these areas, UNCTAD, through its Division on Investment, Technology and Enterprise Development (DITE), promotes the understanding of, and helps build consensus on, matters related to foreign direct investment, transfer of technology and development. DITE also assists developing countries to attract and benefit from FDI and in building their productive capacities and international competitiveness. The emphasis is on an integrated policy approach to investment, technological capacity building and enterprise development.

The term "country" as used in this publication also refers, as appropriate, to territories or areas; the designations employed and the presentation of the material do not imply the expression of any opinion whatsoever on the part of the Secretariat of the United Nations concerning the legal status of any country, territory, city or area or of its authorities, or concerning the delimitation of its frontiers or boundaries. In addition, the designations of country groups are intended solely for statistical or analytical convenience and do not necessarily express a judgement about the stage of development reached by a particular country or area in the development process. The reference to a company and its activities should not be construed as an endorsement by UNCTAD of the company or its activities.

The following symbols are applicable to tables:

- Two dots (.) indicate that data are not available or are not separately reported. Rows in tables have been omitted in those cases where no data are available for any of the elements in the row;
- A dash (-) indicates that the item is equal to zero or its value is negligible;
- A blank in a table indicates that the item is not applicable, unless otherwise indicated;

- A slash (/) between dates representing years, e.g., 1994/95, indicates a financial year;
- Use of a hyphen (-) between dates representing years, e.g., 1994-1995, signifies the full period involved, including the beginning and end years;
- Reference to "dollars" ($) means United States dollars, unless otherwise indicated;
- Annual rates of growth or change, unless otherwise stated, refer to annual compound rates;
- Details and percentages in tables do not necessarily add to totals because of rounding.

The material contained in this study may be freely quoted with appropriate acknowledgement.

The photographs on the cover page are courtesy of Gunter Fischer.

UNCTAD/ITE/IIA/2005/6

UNITED NATIONS PUBLICATION
Sales No. E.06.II.D.2
ISBN 92-1-112694-0

Copyright © United Nations, 2005
All rights reserved
Printed in Switzerland

ACKNOWLEDGEMENT

This publication was edited by Kálmán Kalotay, Thomas Pollan and Torbjörn Fredriksson, under the supervision of Anne Miroux. It was copy edited by Trevor Griffiths. Desktop publishing was done by Teresita Ventura. The cover page was designed by Diego Oyarzun-Reyes.

The secretariat is grateful to the authors of the papers included in this volume, which were presented at the Expert Meeting on "The Impact of FDI on Development", that was held in Geneva from 24 to 26 January 2005 and dealt with the globalization of research and development and its implications for development. These issues are expected to remain for a long time at the heart of policy debate on technological development in developing countries. It is hoped that this volume will contribute to that debate in a timely manner. With the exception of the Overview, which was prepared by the UNCTAD Secretariat, the views and the opinions expressed are those of the authors and not of the United Nations.

CONTENTS

Part III. Policy issues

Part IV. Comments

* * * * * *

PREFACE

Reflecting a broader trend towards the offshoring of services, a number of developing countries are attracting foreign direct investment in research and development. Transnational corporations, including the ones headquartered in developing countries, are selecting developing countries as locations for such activities. With the offshoring of research and development, firms aim to access the skills of new locations, adapting products to local markets and reducing their costs, in response to competitive pressures, technological changes and a more liberal trade and investment environment. In particular, information and communication technologies have had a profound effect on the way economic activities, including research and development, are organized, enabling firms to allocate tasks on a global scale through intra-firm information networks. At the same time, keeping up with new developments in information and communication technologies is a major challenge for developing countries wishing to accelerate their economic development. How important is this relatively recent phenomenon? Is it set to continue?

This publication aims to elaborate key issues related to the trends towards globalization of research and development and their implications for developing countries: What is its development potential? How can the establishment of research and development abroad affect the transfer of technology – one of the main potential benefits from foreign direct investment? What types of research and development are the most desirable for development? What benefits and costs are involved and, how can policies in home and host countries influence the allocation of such activities and their economic impact?

These questions were elaborated at the Expert Meeting on FDI in R&D held in January 2005. This volume contains written submissions presented by scholars and experts at the Expert Meeting. The overview chapter is based on a note prepared by the UNCTAD secretariat for the meeting. The Chairperson's summary of the discussion at the Expert Meeting is also included, reflecting the diversified views expressed by scholars and experts from governments. The issues addressed, to mention a few, included the use of foreign direct investment versus contractual channels in acquiring innovative capacities in developing countries, the potential links of transnational corporations' research and development activities with the local innovation systems of host countries, the likelihood of research and development activities spreading to new developing locations and, the kinds of host country policies that can facilitate the diffusion of technologies from foreign affiliates' activities to the local economy.

UNCTAD's analysis of transnational corporations' research and development activities in developing countries benefited largely from the insights gained at the expert meeting. The continuation and deepening of that analysis resulted in the publication, in September 2005, of the *World Investment Report 2005: Transnational Corporations and the Internationalization of R&D* (*WIR05*; UNCTAD 2005). The readers of this volume may find in *WIR05* a rich body of additional first-hand information on trends in research and development, its development impact and policy implications. Furthermore, readers familiar with the *WIR05* will also find interesting expert opinions and additional case studies.

An overview of the issues[1]

UNCTAD secretariat

For decades, technological change and innovation, driven by research and development (R&D; for a definition, see box 1), have been the most important sources of productivity growth and increased welfare (Edquist 2000). As a result, there is a high correlation between those countries that have shown significant economic improvement in the past and those countries that have made substantial investment in R&D. For that reason, it is imperative for developing countries, including least developed countries (LDCs), to build R&D capacities, without which they are likely to miss opportunities to upgrade their technologies, move up the development ladder and, catch up with developed countries.[2]

Box 1. Definition of R&D

Research and development (R&D) consists of four types of activities: basic and applied research, and product and process development. *Basic research* is original experimental work without a specific commercial aim, frequently done by universities. *Applied research* is original experimental work with a specific aim. *Product development* is the improvement and extension of existing products. *Process development* is the creation of new or improved processes.

Source: UNCTAD.

---

[1] This overview is based on the note by the UNCTAD secretariat on "The impact of FDI on development: globalization of R&D by transnational corporations and implications for developing countries" (TD/B/COM.2/EM.16/2), prepared for the UNCTAD Expert Meeting on FDI in R&D.

[2] Many of the challenges that countries in transition face in R&D are similar to those of developing countries. However, this overview will not discuss in detail the specific situation of countries in transition.

Since transnational corporations (TNCs) are playing a major role in global R&D, it is timely to look at the opportunities and risks that such a process creates for developing countries. In addition to being a source of finance for R&D, TNCs could also help developing countries to build up their R&D commercialization systems by facilitating their access to global supply and distribution chains and external markets. Thus, FDI can serve as a "vehicle for carrying tacit knowledge as well as assisting enterprises at the frontiers of world technological learning" (Liu and Wang 2003: 945).

In certain cases, technology transfer requires the presence of TNCs or their affiliates. Even if technologies are imported, a certain amount of R&D capacity may be necessary in the host economy for absorbing them, adapting them to local conditions and applying them to alternative uses. Moreover, entry barriers to emerging industries, in terms of capital requirements and industrial experience, are low in the initial stages. It is then easier for developing countries to enter and build competitive strength as the technology evolves (e.g. biotechnology). Once an industry reaches consolidation, entry barriers rise (e.g. semiconductors), and developing countries get confined to lower-value-added activities. Another reason why developing countries are paying more attention to this area is that their own firms are also undertaking R&D-related FDI in both developed and developing countries in their quest to acquire and develop R&D capacities. This further underlines the importance of exploring the globalization of R&D and its implications for developing countries.

The participation of developing countries in the globalization of R&D has so far been uneven. On the one hand, some developing countries with robust infrastructures, highly trained workforces, reasonable intellectual property protection and appealing domestic markets – especially in Asia and the Pacific – have attracted significant FDI in R&D (UNCTAD 2005, Pearce 1999). These developing countries have benefited from the opportunities provided by the increasing demand of TNCs for inexpensive talent and for new developing markets. Their policies have focused on measures to maximize the degree of technology spillovers from FDI and, to enhance their absorptive capacity by encouraging local firms to engage in R&D. On the other hand, many other developing countries have fared moderately in growth and welfare creation because their R&D efforts have remained underfunded and delinked from the private sector.

1. Emerging patterns and drivers of the globalization of R&D

a. Trends in R&D by transnational corporations

FDI and technology transfer are increasingly interlinked. TNCs are responsible for a large share of global R&D activities. In 2002, the largest 700 firms worldwide in this area spent $311 billion on R&D (according to data available from the United Kingdom's Department of Trade and Industry). Moreover, in the current global environment characterized by rapidly changing technologies and shorter product life cycles, TNCs are offshoring (box 2) more and more R&D in different parts of the world (Cantwell and Janne 1999) through both FDI and technology alliances (non-equity mode).[3] This pattern of locating R&D differs radically from that of the past (the 1950s and 1960s)[4] and challenges the traditional view that R&D activities by TNCs are undertaken mainly at home. While in itself the expansion of R&D beyond the borders of home countries of TNCs is not a new phenomenon,[5] the scale of

---

[3] Such R&D activities can be part of the manufacturing units or independent R&D laboratories.

[4] During that period, TNCs derived competitive advantages, particularly technological knowledge, from their distinctive domestic environments, which led to the exploitation of this advantage abroad through exports and outward FDI (Hymer 1960; Vernon 1966).

[5] It has been well documented in developed countries in a number of studies (Brash 1966 for Australia; Safarian 1966 for Canada;

offshoring is rising and its geographical reach is spreading to developing countries. The spread of R&D-related FDI to new host countries is part of the broader phenomenon of offshoring services, which is a still relatively new but rising trend (box 2). Within the range of offshored services, R&D represents the higher end of the value-added spectrum.

Box 2. Definition of offshoring and outsourcing

Offshoring is defined as the location or transfer of activities abroad. It can be done internally by moving services from a parent company to its foreign affiliates (sometimes referred to as "captive offshoring", involving FDI, in differentiation from offshoring to third parties). It is different from the concept of outsourcing, which always involves a third party, but not necessarily a transfer abroad. Offshoring and outsourcing overlap only when the activities in question are outsourced internationally to third-party services providers as shown in the table below.

Offshoring and outsourcing R&D: definitions

Location of R&D	Internalized	Externalized ("*Outsourcing*")
Home country	R&D kept in-house at home	R&D outsourced to third party provider at home
Foreign country ("*offshoring*")	R&D by a foreign affiliate of the same TNC, called "*captive offshoring*"	R&D outsourced to a third-party provider abroad: To a *local company* To a *foreign affiliate of another TNC*

Source: UNCTAD, adapted from UNCTAD 2004b: 148.

Stubenitsky 1970 for the Netherlands; Ronstadt 1977 for the United States; Behrman and Fischer 1980 for United States-based and European TNCs; Zander 1994 for Swedish TNCs; Kuemmerle 1999 for various developed countries).

The offshoring of R&D in developing-country locations has involved internationally known TNCs such as Ericsson, GE, IBM, Intel, Microsoft, Motorola, Nokia, Oracle, Texas Instruments and SAP.[6] Data on the activities of the affiliates of TNCs from the Triad (the United States, Japan and the European Union) confirm the rise of corporate R&D in developing countries, although at different speeds. Between 1989 and 1999, R&D performed by all foreign affiliates of United States TNCs in developing countries increased nine times, to $2.4 billion, as compared to a three-fold increase worldwide, to $18 billion in 1999.[7] In developing Asia, there was an 18-fold leap forward to $1.4 billion in 1999.[8] Over the same period (1989–1999), R&D expenditures by Japanese foreign affiliates rose even more rapidly (eight times) than those by United States affiliates, and offshoring of R&D by Japanese TNCs to developing countries grew faster (10 times) than their R&D expenditures worldwide. The offshoring of R&D by European TNCs, especially to developing countries, is still in a nascent stage (Cantwell and Janne, 2000). For example, the outward FDI stock of Germany in R&D amounted to only $970 million at the end of 2002, although this was up from its 1995 level ($43 million).[9] The industry and geographical composition of such R&D is fairly conservative: 97% is spent in manufacturing, and more than 90% takes place in the United States and Europe.

---

[6] For example, in 2004 Intel employed some 1,500 information technology (IT) professionals in India, and Motorola operated one of the largest foreign-owned R&D institutes in China, employing almost 2,000 people.

[7] According to data from the United States Department of Commerce, Bureau of Economic Analysis.

[8] Despite the fact that those statistics may underestimate the role of such locations as India, for which only $20 million, or 0.1% of outward FDI, is reported.

[9] According to unpublished data of the Deutsche Bundesbank.

Reflecting the increased internationalization of R&D, foreign affiliates are assuming more important roles in many host countries' R&D activities. Between 1993 and 2002 the R&D expenditure of foreign affiliates worldwide climbed from an estimated $30 billion to $67 billion (or from 10% to 16% of global business R&D; UNCTAD 2005: 125). Whereas the rise was relatively modest in developed host countries, it was quite significant in developing countries: the share of foreign affiliates in business R&D in the developing world increased from 2% to 18% between 1996 and 2002. The share of R&D by foreign affiliates in different countries varies considerably. In 2003 foreign affiliates accounted for more than half of all business R&D in Ireland, Hungary and Singapore and about 40% in Australia, Brazil, the Czech Republic, Sweden and the United Kingdom. Conversely, it remained under 10% in Chile, Greece, India, Japan and the Republic of Korea (*idem*).

Data on the geographical distribution of foreign affiliates engaged in R&D worldwide (table 1) also point to the growing importance of developing economies. In 2004, of the more than 2,500 affiliates registered in the *Who Owns Whom* database of Dun and Bradstreet, more than 10% were located in developing countries, with developing Asia alone accounting for more than 8%.[10]

Recent data on greenfield R&D projects initiated worldwide also indicate a rise of developing destinations and service-related R&D (OCO Consulting, LOCOmonitor database). Of the more than 1,000 FDI projects in R&D worldwide for which information has been collected for the period August 2002–July 2004, the majority (739) were located in developing countries or economies in transition. Developing Asia and the Pacific alone accounted for more than half of the

---

[10] Furthermore, there are indications that this sample survey underestimates the role of certain Asian locations such as India or the Republic of Korea because of, among other reasons, a classification problem of software development.

world total (563 projects). These data also suggest that the majority of the new jobs created in greenfield R&D projects also went to developing countries, mostly to India and China and, to information and communication technologies (ICT).

Table 1. Geographical distribution of R&D foreign affiliates,[a] 2004
(Number of affiliates)

Region/economy	Number
Total world	**2 584**
Developed countries	**2 185**
of which Western Europe	1 387
United States	552
Japan	29
Developing countries	**264**
of which Africa	4
Latin America and the Caribbean	40
Asia	216
South, East and South-East Asia	207

Source: UNCTAD, based on the *Who Owns Whom* database (Dun and Bradstreet).

[a] On the basis of 2,284 majority-owned foreign affiliates identified in the above database that are engaged in commercial, physical and educational research (SIC code 8731), commercial economics and biological research (SIC code 8732), non-commercial research (SIC code 8733) and testing laboratories (SIC code 8734).

However, FDI data are imperfect indicators of the R&D activities of TNCs abroad. Indeed, firms also often use non-FDI forms such as technology alliances, R&D joint ventures, R&D consortia and university-industry linkages to access strategic knowledge abroad (UNCTAD 2000). These forms of cooperation can be equity- or non-equity based; in most cases they fall outside the scope of the definition of FDI. As part of their alliances, TNCs are outsourcing some technology development activities to firms and research institutes worldwide, including those located in developing countries.

While R&D by TNCs in the developing world is concentrated in a handful of key host economies such as Brazil,

China, Hong Kong (China), India, Mexico, Singapore and South Africa, other countries have also started appearing on the radar screen of TNCs. For example, in 2003 Toyota Motor Corporation (Japan) expanded its R&D activities to Thailand; Monterey Design Systems (United States, software) chose Armenia for a new R&D centre; the IT company SAA Technology (United Kingdom) established an Enterprise Development Centre in Nigeria; and Honda Motor Co. (Japan) set up a new R&D unit in Viet Nam to enhance local motorcycle development and sales.[11] TNCs also target with their agricultural R&D activities some developing countries that are otherwise less prominent on the global R&D scene. This is the case of Kenya, for instance (box 3).

The trend towards the internationalization of R&D activities by TNCs, with particularly fast expansion in developing countries, has been illustrated in a recent survey, in which 70% of the respondents stated that they already had R&D staff abroad and 22% reported conducting some applied research in overseas developing markets. More than half of the respondents were planning to increase their overseas R&D investment (EIU 2004). The top 10 destinations included China (in first position), India (third) and Brazil (sixth). The next 10 on the list included three developing economies: Hong Kong (China) (thirteenth), Mexico and Singapore (sharing fourteenth place).

Recently, a growing number of developing-country TNCs have established R&D activities abroad. While some of them have targeted the knowledge base of developed countries such as the United States, an increasing number have also located their foreign R&D activities in other developing countries. A number of firms from the Republic of Korea, Malaysia, Singapore and Thailand have invested in R&D activities in India, particularly in software-related R&D (Reddy

---

[11] www.ipaworld.com.

2000: 97–103). More recently (in 2003), firms from India, Indonesia and the Republic of Korea for instance, have invested or announced plans to invest also in locations such as Abu Dhabi, China and Singapore.[12]

Box 3. R&D by TNCs in Kenya's agriculture

In general, Kenya is not a major player in global R&D. In agriculture, which generates a large share of its export earnings, R&D expenditures represented only slightly more than 1% of the developing countries' total in 2000.[a] Moreover, the private sector made up only 3% of Kenya's total agricultural R&D expenditure in the same year.[a]

However, there are several agricultural/horticultural or related firms, including TNCs, conducting some form of R&D in Kenya. The known cases of R&D by TNCs in Kenya have followed different strategies. Some TNCs have decided to conduct in-house R&D. Examples include De Ruiter's, Regina Seeds, Fourteen Flowers (Netherlands), Del Monte (United States) and Kordes & Söhne (Germany). Other TNCs, such as East African Breweries (United Kingdom), Monsanto (United States) and Syngenta (Switzerland), have opted for collaborative arrangements with local and foreign partners. The Kenyan Agricultural Research Institute (KARI) carries out research on barley on behalf of East Africa Breweries and works for Syngenta to develop insect-resistant maize for Africa. Monsanto's involvement in Kenyan R&D is more indirect, as its project, originally initiated in direct collaboration with KARI and the International Service for the Acquisition of Agri-tech Applications (ISAAA), has been transferred to its United States non-profit partner Donald Danforth Plant Science Center.[b]

Sources: UNCTAD, CGIAR, ASTI Database (www.asti.cgiar.org/expenditures.cfm) and Beintema and Pardey (2001).
[a] The share of private firms in Kenyan agricultural R&D may be higher, because the original sample was based on information available on three firms only.
[b] The non-profit Donald Danforth Plant Science Center is a partnership organization of the Monsanto Company and various United States-based academic research institutions.

---

[12] See www.ipaworld.com.

b. The drivers

The rise of corporate R&D abroad and the growing importance of some developing economies as locations for R&D-related FDI reflect the combined impact of the global economic environment (global competition), technological progress and improved policy environments.

In the global economic environment, a number of important changes have taken place. First, the technology intensity of products and services has increased significantly, making technology a key factor of competitiveness. Second, the complexities of global competition have increased with the advent of new, more differentiated products and producers, resulting in a need for faster innovation. Third, at a time when the technology intensity of products is increasing and the life cycles of products are shortening, R&D costs are becoming higher. More R&D costs need to be recouped by marketing products as widely as possible. That competitive pressure has opened the door to global product (and R&D) mandates within the corporate networks of TNCs.

Technological change has had a strong impact on the design and organizational patterns of R&D, leading to a proliferation and differentiation of corporate R&D units (box 4). Products have become "modular"[13] as "component interfaces are standardized and interdependencies amongst components are decoupled" (Prencipe et al. 2003: 85), allowing for the fragmentation of design and the specialization of knowledge creation in internal or external networks of TNCs. In addition, the emergence of new science-based technologies (e.g. electronics, ICT, biotechnology and new materials) has had a

---

[13] Modularity is a general property of complex systems, including R&D, innovation and transnational production. These systems are decomposable, at varying degrees, into loosely related subparts and tightly interrelated components.

Box 4. Types of R&D units

Technology transfer units are closely linked to manufacturing units and are established to adapt a parent's products and processes to local conditions in host countries.

Indigenous technology units are set up to develop new and/or improved products for local markets. They are often established when an affiliate identifies locally distinctive investment opportunities and convinces the parent company of its ability to implement such new product development.

Regional technology units are established to develop new and/or improved products for regional markets. These units serve the national markets in regional clusters that share some common features and needs for specialized products.

Global technology units are set up when a single product is envisaged for the global market. This applies, in particular, to two cases: (i) when a TNC has allocated parts of the product range to specific affiliates abroad and may also find it beneficial to carry out R&D relevant to that product range in the same place; (ii) when, because of the magnitude of resources required to develop a product range, it is more efficient for the firm to organize a decentralized but integrated R&D programme.

Corporate technology units are established to generate new technologies of a long-term or exploratory nature exclusively for the parent company in order to protect and enhance the future competitiveness of the company.

Sources: UNCTAD, based on Ronstadt, 1977; and Reddy and Sigurdson, 1994.

---

profound effect on the way economic activities, including R&D, are organized by TNCs (Cantwell and Santangelo 1999). The development of ICT has enabled companies to allocate tasks on a global scale through intra-firm information networks. The emergence of new technologies requiring less industrial experience has also created catching-up opportunities for developing countries with reserves of scientists and engineers. R&D in microelectronics, biotechnology, pharmaceuticals, chemicals and software development can be globalized more easily than R&D in conventional industries, as it can be geographically delinked from production. Moreover, in these new technologies, R&D itself is divisible into different modules, and these may be carried out in different locations. This facilitates the division of R&D into "core" and "non-core" activities. Some of these non-core activities can be carried out in low-cost countries or contracted out to other firms (Reddy 2000).

Improved host country environments have facilitated the globalization of R&D by TNCs. One set of policies in host economies has dealt with the economic bases of R&D activities in general, such as skills and capabilities development, the strengthening of supplier networks, the improvement of infrastructure and the development of science and research bases. Over the decades, some developing countries have trained a sizable number of scientists and engineers, sometimes at advanced levels. Various developing countries have also improved their infrastructure, education and innovative capability, which has placed them on the list of potential host countries for R&D location. They have similarly increased their R&D investment as a proportion of the gross domestic product (GDP).[14] Academic institutions in developing countries have established linkages with their counterparts in developed countries through exchanges and joint research projects, thus strengthening their knowledge base. In addition, the liberalization of trade and investment regimes over the past two decades has also contributed to the globalization of R&D by TNCs.

---

[14] For example, R&D expenditures as a percentage of GDP for the Republic of Korea (2.6% in 2002) were higher than in many developed countries.

2. Implications for development

Opinions differ on the degree to which TNCs' R&D activities help in building up local technological capacity in a host country. On one hand, R&D-related FDI can directly benefit economic growth by stimulating, through the R&D activity undertaken by TNC affiliates, technological efficiency and technological change. The globalization of R&D by TNCs and their location in developing countries may result in what is often believed to be a desirable form of economic activities, to be sought actively by host countries. As TNCs gain control of a growing part of key knowledge and technology in new industries, such as microelectronics, biotechnology, pharmaceuticals, chemicals and software development, the scope for host countries to access them through contractual forms, as selected Asian countries (Japan, the Republic of Korea) did in the twentieth century, may be reduced. However, it still appears possible to rely on a combination of equity and non-equity relations with TNCs.

The potential direct benefits of R&D-related FDI for host countries depend on the mandate and role of different R&D units (box 4). Technology transfer units can most often provide products and processes that are better suited to local conditions and contribute to training local technical staff. Indigenous technology units often provide products that are better suited to local needs and tastes. They can make better use of locally available materials, leading to more cost-effective products and, they have more potential to form linkages with the local innovation system. Regional technology units can establish strong links with the local innovation system, widening its capabilities and, they can help in the international specialization of scientific and technological capabilities. Global technology units and corporate technology units can transfer application knowledge to convert theoretical knowledge into tangible products and processes.

Host economies can also derive direct benefits from TNCs' R&D units through, for instance, (a) subcontracting and sponsorship of research to local universities, and (b) licensing technologies for by-products to local firms. TNCs' R&D activities can also affect the employment prospects of trained people in host economies. Inflows of foreign R&D may help counteract the risk of brain drain from developing countries by providing more job opportunities for skilled people, especially in cases when local capabilities (firms and institutions) cannot create the amount and type of jobs that would respond to the needs and expectations of the local trained workforce. They may also help bring skills back to an economy (e.g. in Ireland or Taiwan Province of China in the past or, in India today).

In some cases TNCs may contribute indirectly to upgrading technologies as innovations emerge and consumption patterns change. The potential spillover effects of TNCs' R&D activities could be categorized as follows:

• The encouragement of commercial culture among scientists and engineers. When R&D-related FDI started flowing into India for instance, scientists in many research institutes started focusing on patentable research. Many of them have become entrepreneurs by forming start-up companies.

• The implantation of an R&D and innovation culture among local companies. For example, TNCs' R&D activities in India spurred an R&D drive among Indian companies, whose R&D expenditures and patenting activities have increased significantly in recent years. Some of these companies (e.g. software companies) compete directly with TNCs.

• The inflow of manufacturing-related FDI to commercialize R&D results at the same location if other conducive parameters are in place.

- Employee spin-offs of R&D companies.[15]

Central to the debate on the spillover impact of TNCs' R&D activities on host economies is the question of whether knowledge and skills can be isolated from their surrounding host environment in the long term. For some observers, the mobility of research personnel and the need for local procurement of staff, material and services are bound to diffuse technologies into the local economy.

On the other hand, the benefits from attracting R&D activities are far from automatic. In fact, in many situations, they may be limited if the foreign affiliates create too few or no local linkages to domestic actors. TNCs' R&D units sometimes create high-technology enclaves with little diffusion of knowledge into the economy. Moreover, with the fragmentation of R&D and the increasing specialization of individual units, the scope for transferring broad knowledge may be narrowing, reinforcing the enclave nature of R&D units.

In addition, when investment into the R&D facility takes the form of a merger and acquisition, it may be argued that such transactions entail a simple change of ownership, akin to portfolio investment, with lesser developmental value. Some take-overs could have an adverse effect on local innovatory capacities, as was illustrated in the 1990s by the acquisition of firms in the automotive and telecommunications industries of Brazil by TNCs. In this case, the result was a scaling down of R&D activities in the acquired firms (UNCTAD 1999).

FDI into R&D may also divert scarce local R&D resources of host countries from local firms and research institutions. For instance, FDI may attract the best R&D personnel. It may also result in a high opportunity cost when

---

[15] For instance, an engineer working at Hewlett Packard started an R&D company called Parallax Research in Singapore. This company now develops products for Hewlett Packard (Reddy 2000).

scarce public resources are diverted to foreign affiliates at the expense of local firms and institutions. TNCs may also show more propensity to transfer the results of innovation performed in developed countries than to transfer the innovation process itself (UNCTAD 1999). These innovations may not benefit manufacturing and marketing operations in the host country, except in that its personnel would be more prestigious and creative (Pearce 1989).

Finally, the geographical concentration of corporate R&D in a handful of host countries within the developing world may raise concerns about the marginalization of the rest of the developing world in the emerging global knowledge society. Without an adequate science and technology base, attracting corporate R&D and benefiting from it could remain a challenge for the majority of developing countries, rather than an opportunity. Weighting the opportunity costs of an R&D policy against the risks of further marginalization and an increased R&D gap is a matter of debate for policy makers. However, the changing nature of R&D, and in particular the fragmentation of R&D activities by TNCs, could open up opportunities to a number of developing countries. All R&D is not necessarily at the higher end of the value chain. With the modularization of R&D by TNCs, some smaller developing countries for instance, could specialize in niche areas to fit into the global knowledge networks developing around TNCs.

3. Policy environment to promote R&D-related FDI and its benefits

a. Host country measures

The ability to attract and benefit from R&D-related FDI depends to a large extent on the policy environment in the host country. A stable and good general policy environment, including macro-economic and political stability, as well as consistent and transparent investment, trade and industrial policies, are important. Good communication systems and other infrastructural facilities are equally important for the dispersed R&D activities of TNCs. Developing countries may have to improve their ICT infrastructure (e.g. access to the Internet). Furthermore, a well-developed national innovation system (NIS) – a "network of institutions in the public and private sectors whose activities and interactions initiate, import, modify and diffuse new technologies" (Freeman 1987: 1) – can facilitate the clustering of economic agents in a given host economy, including foreign affiliates, local firms, and local research institutions. Hence, specific policies may be required to improve the availability of local universities, professionals and researchers (particularly important for global technology units), to create and nurture local knowledge development and, improve the attractiveness of the sources of technical excellence (e.g. universities, suppliers) (de Meyer and Mizushima 1989).

Since TNCs tend to locate R&D in countries where there are reputed academic institutions, a major challenge for the national innovation policies of developing countries is to strengthen their academic establishments by recruiting adequate staff and providing them with adequate funding to carry out research. Universities should also be able to provide doctoral- and post-doctoral-level education in science and technology subjects. Such capacity building can take place for instance, through partnership with the private sector. The participation of senior managers from both domestic and foreign firms in the governing boards of the academic institutions can be one way of strengthening such linkages by making the research more relevant to the industry (Reddy 2000).

In science-based technologies, the difference between basic research and applied research is not always clear-cut. At least some innovation activities in these technologies can be carried out in academic laboratories. Many governments have established R&D centres to promote the technological upgrading of firms. In order to enhance the innovation capability and economic benefits through university-industry collaboration, the establishment of science parks may be important. Such parks may attract both local firms and TNCs to locate R&D, if the parks are established in proximity to reputed academic establishments and the staff in these academic institutions has the freedom to collaborate with enterprises (Reddy 2000). Some of the parks and business incubators, such as the Hsinchu Science Park in Taiwan Province of China and the Magnet Program in Israel, have been quite successful (World Bank 2004: 173). However, when the dynamic interplay of entrepreneurship, R&D institutions, skilled labour, capital, and infrastructure is missing, the results are more mixed (Feser 2002, de Ferranti et al. 2003).

Performance requirements – either mandatory or voluntary – have been used by policy makers in various countries to maximize benefits from FDI (UNCTAD 2003). They have been used in particular to address concerns that excessive reliance on FDI could limit technological development, since R&D was perceived to be largely concentrated in home countries. However, mandatory applications of R&D requirements appear to be rare. It is more common to link R&D criteria to the receipt of various kinds of incentives – these are the so-called voluntary performance requirements (e.g. in Chile, Malaysia and South Africa, as well as in several developed countries). However, the results have often been limited because a firm is unlikely to set up R&D activities in the absence of local capabilities and technical skills to absorb, adapt and develop technology and know-how. Furthermore, performance requirements may carry the potential risk of losing would-be investors not wishing to comply with those criteria.

In the area of fiscal incentives, Brazil applies a scheme in which companies that invest in R&D are levied a reduced tax on imported products (EIU 2004: 13). India, Malaysia, Mexico, the Republic of Korea, South Africa and Taiwan Province of

China are other salient cases of developing economies' providing fiscal incentives to R&D (table 2).[16] Some developing countries have also used financial market interventions to encourage firms to pursue R&D, including directed credit schemes (Republic of Korea) and venture capital funds (Malaysia) (Kim 1997 and Yusuf 2003, respectively). Some studies have found evidence that R&D incentives were cost-effective (Shah and Baffes 1995, for Pakistan; and Shah 1995, for Canada). However, the literature on tax incentives in the developed countries[17] shows more mixed results in the majority of the cases analysed. The main reason for these findings is that in comparison with the availability and quality of appropriately skilled labour, the provision of fiscal or financial incentives is of limited relevance for R&D investments.

Table 2. Fiscal incentives for R&D in selected developing economies, 2004
(Percentage)

Economy	R&D depreciation	R&D capital depreciation	Tax credit
Brazil	100	100	None
India	100	100	None
Malaysia	200	Same as other investment	None
Mexico	100	3 years' straight-line depreciation	None
Republic of Korea	100	18–20	10–25
South Africa	100	25	None
Taiwan Province of China	100	Same as other investment	15–20

Source: UNCTAD, based on World Bank (2004: 173).

---

[16] In this respect, they are following the example of some developed countries, such as the United States, Australia, Canada, France, Japan and the Netherlands, which offer tax credits, full expensing of R&D and even double deductions of some R&D spending (World Bank 2004: 178).

[17] See Hall and Van Reenen 1999 for a literature review.

One of the specific policy areas that affect the location of corporate R&D in developing countries is the protection of intellectual property rights (IPRs), which is perceived by some TNCs as a precondition for such locational decisions. According to corporate surveys, the protection of IPR is usually mentioned by some TNCs among the top criteria in taking an R&D investment decision. In a recent survey, 38% of the respondents mentioned IPR as a critically important challenge, a higher proportion than for any other issue (EIU 2004: 5).

b. Home country measures

While host country policies are crucial, measures taken by home countries of TNCs also affect the international allocation of R&D activities. For example, home countries may provide special incentives to their TNCs to locate R&D units in developing countries where such TNCs have assembly or manufacturing plants. They may also provide special tax concessions to their TNCs for R&D investments made in developing countries. The most common home country measures include support for FDI, training, matching services, partnerships and alliances, and support for equipment purchase or licensing (UNCTAD 2004a). For instance, of the 41 programmes and agencies surveyed by UNCTAD in 2004 in 23 countries, 15 provided incentives to their enterprises to enable them to establish R&D in developing countries. Of these, three had a technology transfer fund or a financing mechanism that was independent of FDI support measures (UNCTAD 2004a). This measure directly facilitates transfer of technology, and therefore could also be adopted by other countries.

However, the offshoring of R&D activities may also raise concerns in home countries, in spite of the fact that, in principle, the offshoring of R&D activities should offer benefits to all parties concerned. First, a large part of offshoring R&D activities continues to target developed countries. Slowing down offshoring could deprive such developed countries of FDI opportunities. Second, as noted above, important reasons for firms to expand their R&D activities in lower-cost locations are to access skills and to lower costs. Protectionist measures to obstruct the globalization of R&D may therefore have adverse effects on the competitiveness of the firms involved and, by extension, their home economies. Given the short history of R&D globalization, there is a need for further analysis of its implications for both host and home countries.

c. International dimension

At the international policy level, issues related to FDI in R&D have been addressed in various manners, depending on the nature and purpose of individual international investment agreements (IIAs). The overwhelming majority of those agreements provide protection to foreign affiliates' R&D activities and their related products by defining TNCs' intellectual property as one type of the investment covered by the definition provisions of the respective agreement. These agreements contribute to creating an enabling framework for the globalization of R&D by TNCs. As regards performance requirements, some IIAs prohibit using R&D as a condition for the establishment of an investment, while some others explicitly mention that the agreements do not prevent a party from conditioning the receipt of an advantage in connexion with foreign investment (i.e. an incentive) in compliance with a requirement to carry out R&D.

The WTO Agreement on Trade-Related Intellectual Property Rights (TRIPS Agreement) does not expressly address issues related to FDI in R&D. However, it provides an enabling framework for the protection of R&D activities (including their intellectual inputs and outputs) carried out by foreign affiliates, for instance, by promoting minimum international standards for the protection of IPRs (e.g. patents, copyrights, trademarks, industrial designs and trade secrets). These standards are subject to most-favoured-nation-treatment, national-treatment and domestic-enforcement obligations. Some aspects of these obligations and standards however, may limit developing countries' policy options for promoting the development of domestic innovation capacity. For example, the protection of foreign R&D activities through a patent may limit the possibilities for domestic industry to engage in follow-on innovation (e.g. if the patent is broad and covers elements the domestic third parties would have to rely on for their research).

References

Behrman JN and Fischer WA (1980). *Overseas R&D Activities of Transnational Companies.* Cambridge, MA: Oelgeschlager, Gunn & Hain.

Beintema N and Pardey PG (2001). "Slow magic: Agricultural R&D a century after Mendel". ASTI Initiative, IFPPI. Mimeo.

Brash DT (1966). *American Investment in Australian Industry* Canberra: Australian National University Press.

Cantwell J and Janne O (1999). "Technological globalisation and innovative centres: The role of corporate technological leadership and locational hierarchy", *Research Policy* 28: 119–144.

_____ (2000). "The role of multinational corporations and national states in the globalisation of innovatory capacity: The European perspective", *Technology Analysis and Strategic Management* 12 (2): 243–262.

Cantwell J and Santangelo GD (1999). "The frontier of international technology networks: Sourcing abroad the most highly tacit capabilities", *Information Economics and Policy* 11: 101–123.

de Ferranti D, Perry GE, Gill IS, Guasch JL, Maloney WF, Sanchez-Paramo C and Schady N (2003). *Closing the Gap in Education and Technology.* Washington, D.C.: World Bank.

de Meyer A and Mizushima A (1989). "Global R&D management", *R&D Management* 19 (2): 135– 146.

Economist Intelligence Unit (EIU) (2004). "Scattering the seeds of invention: The globalisation of research and development". London: EIU. http://graphics.eiu.com/files/ad_pdfs/RnD_GLOBILISATION_WH ITEPAPER.pdf.

Edquist C (2000). "Systems of innovation approaches – their emergence and characteristics". In Edquist C and McKelvey M, eds., *Systems of Innovation: Growth, Competitiveness and Employment.* Cheltenham, UK: Edward Elgar.

Feser E (2002). "The relevance of clusters for innovation policy in Latin America and the Caribbean". Background paper prepared for the World Bank, LAC group. Washington, D.C.: World Bank. Mimeo.

Freeman C (1987). *Technology and Economic Performance: Lessons from Japan.* London: Pinter.

Hall BH and Van Reenen J (1999). "How effective are fiscal incentives for R&D? A review of the evidence", *Research Policy* 29 (4–5): 449–469.

Hymer SH (1960). "The international operations of national firms: a study of direct foreign investment". Massachusetts Institute of Technology, Cambridge, MA, Ph.D. thesis.

Kim L (1997). *Imitation to Innovation: the Dynamics of Korea's Technological Learning.* Cambridge, MA: Harvard Business School Press.

Kuemmerle W (1999). "Foreign direct investment in industrial research in the pharmaceutical and electronics industries – results from a survey of multinational firms", *Research Policy* 28 (2– 3): 179–193.

Liu X and Wang C (2003). "Does foreign direct investment facilitate technological progress? Evidence from Chinese industries", *Research Policy* 32: 945–953.

Pearce RD (1989). *The Internationalisation of Research and Development by Multinational Enterprises.* London: Macmillan.

_____ (1999). "Decentralised R&D and strategic competitiveness: Globalised approaches to generation and use of technology in multinational enterprises (MNEs)", *Research Policy* 28: 157–178.

Prencipe A, Davies A and Hobday M (2003). *The Business of Systems Integration.* Oxford: Oxford University Press.

Reddy P (2000). *Globalization of Corporate R&D: Implications for Innovation Systems in Host Countries.* London and New York: Routledge.

_____ and Sigurdson J (1994). "Emerging patterns of globalisation of corporate R&D and scope for innovation capability building in developing countries?", *Science and Public Policy* 21 (5): 283–294.

Ronstadt RC (1977). *Research and Development Abroad by US Multinationals.* New York: Praeger.

Safarian AE (1966). *Foreign Ownership of Canada's Industry.* Toronto: McGraw Hill.

Shah A (1995). "Research and development investment, industrial structure, economic performance, and tax policies". In Shah A, ed., *Fiscal Incentives for Investment and Innovation.* New York: Oxford University Press.

_____ and Baffes J (1995). "Do tax policies stimulate investment in physical and R&D capital? In Shah A, ed., *Fiscal Incentives for Investment and Innovation.* New York: Oxford University Press.

Stubenitsky F (1970). *American Direct Investment in the Netherlands Industry.* Rotterdam: Rotterdam University Press.

UNCTAD (1999). *World Investment Report 1999: Foreign Direct Investment and the Challenge for Development.* New York and Geneva: United Nations. United Nations publication, Sales No. E.99.II.D.3.

_____ (2000).*World Investment Report 2000: Cross-Border Mergers and Acquisitions and Development.* New York and Geneva: United Nations. United Nations publication, Sales No. E.00.II.D.20.

_____ (2003). *Foreign Direct Investment and Performance Requirements: New Evidence from Selected Countries.* New York and Geneva: United Nations. United Nations publication, Sales No. E.03.II.D.32.

_____ (2004a). *Facilitating Transfer of Technology to Developing Countries: A Survey of Home Country Measures.* New York and Geneva: United Nations.

_____ (2004b). *World Investment Report 2004: The Shift towards Services.* New York and Geneva: United Nations. United Nations publication, Sales No. E.04.II.D.36.

_____ (2005). *World Investment Report 2005: Transnational Corporations and the Internationalization of R&D.* New York and Geneva: United Nations. United Nations publication, Sales No. E.05.II.D.10.

Vernon R (1966). "International investment and international trade in the product cycle", *Quarterly Journal of Economics* 82 (2): 190–207.

World Bank (2004). *World Development Report 2005.* Washington, D.C.: World Bank.

Yusuf S (2003). *Innovative East Asia: The Future of Growth.* Washington, D.C.: World Bank.

Zander I (1994). "The tortoise evolution of the multinational corporation: Foreign technological activity in Swedish multinational firms 1890–1990". Institute of International Business, Stockholm, Ph.D. thesis.

PART I

The globalization of R&D

The globalization of R&D: key features and the role of TNCs

Robert Pearce[1]

A commitment to R&D can be seen as logically central to the dynamic developmental needs of both TNCs and individual national economies. Early analysis and evaluation of TNCs and FDI saw the location of R&D as being the developed home countries of these firms and the internationalization of their operations based around processes of outward technology transfer. The immediate developmental implications of this for developing host countries were then seen as relating to the quality of this transferred technology; its appropriateness and the ability of local economies to assimilate and utilize it effectively. The potential for poorer host countries to escape from the implications of such a technological dependency would then be limited to such relatively minor localized adaptations of products and processes as TNCs' competitive needs impelled them to carry out. Beyond this, such early thinking argued, the persistence of an R&D/innovation hegemony of a small group of TNC home countries could impose an inherently non-dynamic hierarchical stratification on the global economy (Hymer 1972).

Perhaps the single most important element in the changing understanding of the practicalities of TNCs' strategic behaviour over the past 30 years or so has been the perception of a breakdown in such an immutable home-country orientation of creative (competitiveness generating) activity and moves towards globalized programmes for innovation and R&D. Thus, the tendency to see TNCs' organizational structures as

---

[1] The views expressed in this study are those of the author and do not necessarily reflect the views of the United Nations, its Member States, or the Institutions to which the author is affiliated.

predominantly hierarchical has been replaced by attempts to analyse them in terms of heterarchy (Hedlund 1986, Birkinshaw 1994) or, as dynamic differentiated networks. This places a decisive emphasis on two factors; TNCs' responses to heterogeneity in the form of various differences between locations (their potential and needs) and a dynamic, ever evolving, structure in their global networks that can alter, quite quickly, how they operate in different countries and regions (from export processing zones to creative knowledge-based clusters).

The aim of this paper is to elaborate on relevant aspects of this strategic restructuring in TNCs, and then provide some detail on how this is operationalized in terms of the increased decentralization of their R&D programmes. The aim of this analysis though, is to provide a basis for discussion of the implications of these more differentiated and dynamic strategic orientations in TNCs for the host countries in which they operate, with particular emphasis on countries at early stages of competitiveness development and, on economies in transition. The strategic changes in TNCs now involve them with creative resources (R&D, technology stocks, market research, entrepreneurial management) in national economies in a way not envisaged 40 years ago. However in doing this do TNCs necessarily strengthen these creative attributes of host countries? Even if they do, does this mean that these creative attributes necessarily improve the competitiveness of the local economy and, thereby, provide a basis for sustainable development or, can TNCs use the flexibility of their global networks to apply new technologies and competitive capacities that are generated in one country, in supply operations in another? When TNCs use R&D and other creative inputs in several locations to support improvements in their global competitiveness, are individual locations that contribute to this fairly rewarded (in terms of improved efficiency and economic growth; Pearce 2002)?

1. Technology/R&D/innovation needs of TNCs

It is useful to characterize the strategic positioning of the contemporary TNC "as one of seeking to use the increasing freedoms of international transfer, reflecting the essence of economic globalization, to leverage the differences between economic areas" (Pearce forthcoming). Three types of diversity or heterogeneity can then be suggested as relevant to the strategic postures of TNCs today.

- Firstly, availabilities of standardized inputs to mature production processes. Differences in these sources of comparative advantage between countries (or regions) can determine which TNC goods are produced where, and therefore patterns of intra-group technology transfer and, possibly, technology adaptation.
- Secondly, differences in demand conditions between countries (i.e. market heterogeneity). An important understanding of the forces of globalization, which has emerged in recent years, is that in many industries and product groups this has not led to demand standardization but often instead, to an increased willingness to manifest localized taste differences. Thus, the in-depth research of Bartlett and Ghoshal (1989) showed that many successful TNCs benefited from a willingness to respond to local taste differentiation, rather than seeking to override it (perhaps in pursuit of economies of scale). In fact, the ability of TNCs to benefit from acknowledgement of market heterogeneity can go beyond willingness to differentiate existing product ranges. Here, especially in industries oriented towards demand-driven innovation processes, it is the unmet wants of customers that can be crucial when accessed by good quality market research. Such ideas for major new products can emerge unpredictably, at any time, in any country at almost any level of income.
- Thirdly, it may be that one of the crucial forces conditioning the patterns of development in the era of

globalization has been a systemic deepening of technological heterogeneity. Thus, increasing numbers of countries have sought to generate the knowledge sources for economic development through commitment of resources to R&D and support of a distinctive NIS. However, analysis has suggested that an outcome of this is that individual national economies have become scientifically and technologically stronger in increasingly differentiated ways. Individual national science-bases have become increasingly specialized, acquiring international leadership in a small and focused range of scientific disciplines, whilst accepting a concomitant relative weakness in many others. Forces of agglomeration, including very notably the R&D and innovation strategies of TNCs to be discussed here, tend to reinforce these patterns of technological and research heterogeneity across the evolving global economy.

Against this background the modern TNC faces, with increasing intensity, two basic competitive pressures. Firstly, the tactical need to supply its established product range in the most cost-effective and market-responsive way possible. Secondly, a complementary need to address forward-looking issues of strategic competitiveness (Pearce 1999), in the sense of securing the new sources of firm-level distinctiveness that can help sustain its position in an inevitably dynamic market environment. We can then suggest that these needs provide the TNC with three levels of competitive priority in the areas of technology application and generation, which are increasingly being pursued through global networks.

As suggested, the immediate short-term priority for TNCs is to achieve the optimally effective and competitive use of their existing technologies, as embodied in successful established goods and services. Crucially this involves being responsive to differences in supply conditions in particular locations in the global economy (i.e. the input heterogeneity noted earlier). Thus, over perhaps the past four decades, the increasing freedom of trade, along with the adoption of export-oriented development strategies in many of the countries that were earlier oriented to import substitution has made it both necessary and feasible for TNCs to implement integrated global supply strategies (Papanastassiou and Pearce 1999, Pearce 2001) and, separate where goods are produced from where they are sold (generating intra-group trade).

In this process, a careful categorization of the different factor needs of different goods can lead to each being allocated to a supply affiliate in the location able to provide the required input mix in the most cost-effective manner. Once a particular affiliate has been allocated supply responsibility for a product, in reflection of the host economy's input potentials, the TNC will then make available all the technical specifications (product characteristics, manufacturing process details, etc) needed to activate its role. Thus, the generation of such a supply network in TNCs places a high priority on effective intra-group mechanisms for technology transfer, assimilation and adaptation.

Nevertheless, however proficient a TNC may be in securing optimal supply and maximized profitability from its current products, it will know that this range will not sustain its competitive position very far into the future. Therefore, it must be continually targeting the medium-term priority of innovation, seeking to add new technological and/or market insights to existing competences in order to secure very significant developments to its competitive scope. Some of the most important insights into the strategic evolution of TNCs in recent years have then related to their increasing acceptance of the decentralization of innovation into globalized operations. Implicit in this is the acceptance of technological and market heterogeneity, indicating that new scientific or customer-driven initiatives towards significant product development can emerge anywhere in a TNC's global operations.

Vital to the decentralization of innovation in TNCs has been the emergence of a new type of affiliate, often designated as a product mandate, which acquires permission from its group parent to take full responsibility for the development of a new good. To accede effectively to this degree of individualized creativity, a product mandate must assemble, from strengths available in its host-country economy, a rich range of functional capabilities. These need to include R&D (to generate, or mediate the acquisition and application of new technologies), market research (to detect unmet market needs and/or to formulate the means of projecting new goods to initial customers), inventive engineering (to establish a prototype production process) and crucially, entrepreneurial affiliate-level management (to drive the integrated creative processes and to provide persistent advocation of the affiliate's status in the group network). By allowing such localized initiatives in product mandates the modern heterarchical (Hedlund 1986) TNCs provide themselves with a means of tapping into the globally dispersed technological and market heterogeneities that drive competitive progress. Here, by contrast with the cost-based supply affiliates, product mandates go through a creative transition (Papanastassiou and Pearce 1999) such that (rather than being allocated existing group technology to play an externally-determined role) it is their own internalized and individualized technology and competences that earn them their position.

Looking into a longer-term future, TNCs should also foresee a need for much more radical changes in competitive scope, based on much more fundamental restructuring of the types of services supplied and the technologies used. In anticipation that such changes are most likely to derive from new science-based possibilities and, in the hope of securing a highly profitable leadership advantage in these discoveries, TNCs may commit resources now to speculative pure-science research in disciplines considered likely to generate relevant breakthroughs. However, to cover a number of potentially relevant areas of science, bearing in mind the narrow national specialisms resulting in the technological heterogeneity observed earlier, ambitious TNCs may need to be involved with basic research programmes in several countries. Covering this aspect of forward-looking competitiveness may again involve internationalized perspectives.

2. Global R&D programmes of TNCs

In order to organize an understanding of the complex strategic positioning of R&D in contemporary TNCs two types of classificatory system have been developed. Firstly, typologies have been derived (Behrman and Fischer 1980, von Zedtwitz and Gassmann 2002) to distinguish different emphases in overall global R&D programmes of TNCs. Secondly, typologies (Ronstadt 1977, Haug, Hood and Young 1983, Medcof, 1997) have been generated to distinguish the different roles played by individual R&D laboratories in TNC networks. Here we use a particular three-part typology (Papanastassiou and Pearce 1999, Pearce 1999 and 2002, Pearce and Singh 1992, Pearce and Papanastassiou 1999).

a. Support laboratories

Support laboratories help achieve the short-run aims of TNCs by securing the effective transfer and application of the group's already successful technologies as embodied in the current product range. As efficiency-seeking TNCs reconfigure global-supply networks and reallocate production responsibility for particular goods to new affiliates, in potentially lower-cost locations, support laboratories facilitate this transfer process by helping these affiliates to assimilate, apply and, where relevant adapt these technologies. This is essentially a static optimization role in that its aim is to allow the TNC to make the most effective use of its current sources of competitiveness and, similarly, secures the greatest value from the activation of the country's sources of static comparative advantage (notably labour). For neither the TNC nor the country does the support laboratory possess any real dynamic potentials, in the sense of providing additional forward-looking dimensions to their sources of competitiveness. Nevertheless, by putting into an affiliate a source of potential individualization (albeit only in terms of improving local ability to play a predetermined role using externally-provided technology) support laboratories may still suggest a creative route forward to a more significant deepening of a localized element in the affiliate's competitiveness.

b. Locally integrated laboratories

The *locally integrated laboratory* becomes a key component of a localized innovation process that is encompassed within a particular affiliate of the product mandate type and, therefore contributes to the way the TNC is pursuing its medium-term objective (i.e. of effective product-range renewal). Whether the innovation is science-driven or demand-driven, the assumption is that it will usually involve either the initial operationalization of completely new technologies, derived from recent scientific breakthroughs or, a substantial reconfiguration of existing ones. The locally integrated laboratory then plays the role of mediating the application of these technologies in closely integrated collaboration with the other key innovation-supporting functions (marketing, engineering, management). A successful nexus between the product mandate and the locally integrated laboratory, through its own distinctive contribution to the TNC's product range, asserts a powerful middle-level position in the group; subject to the continued approval of higher-level decision makers, (validating the mandate) but also possessed of scope for dynamic initiative and capacity to commit resources to speculative creative work.

Though the broad product mandate/locally integrated laboratory position in TNCs plays a demand-side role (in the sense of seeking to fill perceived gaps in the group's current competitive scope) the location of a particular unit of this type also reflects supply-side influences (in the sense that its ability to play the role derives from specific creative inputs-personnel, technologies, etc. – available in its host economy). For the product-mandate/locally-integrated laboratory to then contribute positively to host-country development, two conditions ought to be fulfilled. Firstly, that the local creative inputs co-opted by the TNC are, in the short-run, used more effectively than they would otherwise have been. Secondly, that the product mandate/locally integrated laboratory contributes to further improvements in the capacities and capabilities of these local resources.

With regard to the former it can be suggested that very often when TNC product mandate/locally integrated laboratory operations make use of local skill/technology inputs they combine them with strong group-level attributes (e.g. established technologies, global market perspectives and access) to develop strongly original and competitive new goods (beyond the compass of a purely local enterprise). This then immediately endows the local economy with a new high-employment export-oriented supply capability. However, this may be temporary since, once the product becomes mature and its market more price-competitive, the TNC may reallocate its production to a lower-cost location. This emphasis on the dynamic intra-group competition within TNCs then points toward the second issue. Thus, due to the vulnerability of their dynamic developmental role, product mandate/locally integrated laboratory affiliates need to be looking towards further innovation and improving the creative assets at their disposal to do this. This, in turn, indicates that these TNC operations expect to benefit from progress in the scientific and technological capacity of their host-country and, therefore, will provide support (including R&D collaboration, scientific and other training) for local upgrading in these areas.

c. Internationally interdependent laboratories

In pursuing the longer-term strategic need of TNCs, the internationally independent laboratories are immediately differentiated from support laboratories and locally integrated laboratories by having no concern or connexion whatsoever with the group's currently-operationalized technologies or, with any of its current commercial issues. Instead, an internationally independent laboratory is entirely oriented to pure/basic research in one or more of the scientific disciplines that are considered likely to provide results that can become part of the technological inputs to very radical new product breakthroughs (perhaps reformulating the very nature of the services offered by an industry). Given the narrow focus of the outstanding areas of research leadership of individual countries (technological heterogeneity) and, the often wide range of disciplines that can potentially fuel the technological progress of an industrial sector, a TNC seeking access to top quality investigation in all the relevant areas of science will need to set up internationally independent laboratories in a quite extensive selection of locations. This leads to a network of internationally independent laboratories, each of which follows its own distinctive research agenda, reflecting a specialized area of expertise. But since the expectation is that any new breakthroughs may ultimately derive from synergistic combinations of results from different parts of the network, TNCs will propagate interdependencies between internationally independent laboratories. Thus these laboratories, whilst focusing on clearly defined research of their own, will also share their new insights with, and be prepared to ask questions of, other such units.

Internationally independent laboratories certainly have the potential to reinforce a country's developing strength at the phase of basic research and pure science. They can do this both by providing extra funding and by adding further dimensions to the research by positioning it in the wider technological perspectives of the TNC. However, there is no mechanism by which internationally independent laboratories necessarily strengthen the competitive scope of the host economy. Thus, important results of an internationally independent laboratory feed into the internal technology programmes of parent TNCs and are likely therefore, to contribute to competitiveness generation for the group that need not be activated in the internationally independent laboratory's host country (Pearce 2002).

3. TNC R&D and national development

From an understanding of how TNCs at a point in time build global technological and supply strategies around different roles for laboratories and affiliates, we can also suggest how this can support processes of economic change (development or transition) over time. The various roles taken by laboratories and affiliates reflect different host-country resource potentials, and development (in its very nature) comprises changes in the resource characteristics of economies. Thus, the form of TNCs' involvement with economies can change over time in mutually beneficial and supportive ways.

At the very early stages of a country's development, cost-based TNC operations (perhaps including a support laboratory) can provide a strong impetus to growth by drawing unemployed resources (notably labour) into export-oriented industrial activity. A danger here is that once full-employment is reached labour and other costs will rise, providing a potential for footloose closure (relocation) of the cost-oriented TNC affiliates. A positive possibility here, however, would be for an affiliate to firstly move towards the supply of higher-value parts of the TNC product range (involving inward transfer of more advanced group technologies, again perhaps mediated by a support laboratory) and, eventually accede to product mandate/locally integrated laboratory status (Pearce 2001). This option would clearly be more viable where, in the manner of the newly industrialized Asian economies (Lall 1996), host governments reinvested revenues from early development in improved training, education (including higher education) and commitment to scientific research (ultimately the generation of an NIS). As countries' sources of growth and competitiveness move towards science and technology, the global R&D and innovation strategies of TNCs have the potential to become sustainable embedded components of such knowledge-based development.

Finally, we can note a variant of this scenario that is potentially available to some of the countries in transition from centrally planned economies (Manea and Pearce 2004). During the earlier socialist periods, many of these countries built up strong science bases and quite well trained industrial labour forces. That this had not led to competitive industries, based around local technology and creative capacities, reflected a lack of entrepreneurial risk taking in the absence of market forces. The availability of a stock of creative potentials (technology and human capital) in important emerging market spaces could lead TNCs to very quickly adopt the product mandate/locally integrated laboratory, and even internationally independent laboratory research, in these countries. Here TNC R&D and innovation could provide a short cut through some stages of industrialization-oriented development.

References

Bartlett CA and Ghoshal S (1989). *Managing Across Borders: the Transnational Solution.* London: Hutchinson Business Books.

Behrman JN and Fischer WA (1980). *Overseas R&D Activities of Transnational Companies.* Cambridge, Mass.: Oelgeschlager, Gunn and Hain.

Birkinshaw JM (1994). "Approaching heterarchy – a review of the literature on multinational strategy and structure", *Advances in International Comparative Management* 9: 111-144.

Haug P, Hood N and Young S (1983). "R&D intensity in the affiliates of US-owned electronics companies manufacturing in Scotland", *Regional Studies* 17: 383-392.

Hedlund G (1986). "The hypermodern MNC: a heterarchy?", *Human Resource Management* 25: 9-35.

Hymer SH (1972). "The multinational corporation and the law of uneven development". In Bhagwati JN, ed., *Economics and World Order, From the 1970s to the 1990s*. London: Macmillan: 113-140.

Lall S (1996). *Learning From the Asian Tigers – Studies in Technology and Industrial Policy*. London: Macmillan.

Manea J and Pearce R (2004). "Industrial restructuring in economies in transition and TNCs' investment motivations", *Transnational Corporations* 13(2): 7-27.

Medcof JW (1997). "A taxonomy of internationally dispersed technology units and its application to management issues", *R&D Management* 27(4): 301-318.

Papanastassiou M and Pearce R (1999). *Multinationals, Technology and National Competitiveness*. Cheltenham: Elgar.

Pearce RD (1999). "Decentralised R&D and strategic competitiveness: globalised approaches to generation and use of technology in multinational enterprises", *Research Policy* 28(2-3): 157-178.

_____ (2001). "Multinationals and industrialisation: the bases of inward investment policy", *International Journal of the Economics of Business* 9(1): 51-73.

_____ (2002). "National systems of innovation and the international technology strategies of multinationals, paper presented at the European International Business Academy Conference, Athens.

_____ (forthcoming). "Globalisation and development: an international business strategy approach", *Transnational Corporations* (forthcoming special issue).

_____ and Papanastassiou M (1999). "Overseas R&D and the strategic evolution of MNEs: evidence from laboratories in the UK", *Research Policy* 28(1): 23-41.

_____ and Singh S (1992). *Globalising Research and Development.* London: Macmillan.

Ronstadt RC (1977). *Research and Development Abroad by US Multinationals.* New York: Praeger.

von Zedtwitz, M. and O. Gassmann (2002). "Market versus technology drive in R&D internationalisation: four different patterns of managing research and development", *Research Policy* 31: 569-588

Knowledge creation and why it matters for development: the role of TNCs

Rajneesh Narula[1]

TNCs are one of the key features of globalization and important sources of capital and technology. Perhaps even more importantly, TNCs account for a significant share of global business expenditures in R&D and, present an important *potential* opportunity to promote knowledge creation (of which formal R&D is a subset) in the countries in which they locate. They also represent an alternative to traditional technology transfer approaches to promote the competitiveness of domestic firms in the developing world. The failure of protected industries in developing countries to become competitive in global markets has highlighted the limitations of the arms-length technology transfer approach. At the same time, the need to build strong local capabilities has not diminished. On the contrary, it has risen as increasingly mobile TNCs seek strong complementary factors at sites where they locate.

Hence, in recent years, both governments and supranational organizations have increasingly come to focus on the role TNCs and FDI can play in innovation and knowledge creation. This has been accompanied by a lifting of many types of regulations that previously limited the role of FDI and TNCs in many developing countries, and a reassessment among donors of the role of public versus private actors in development aid.

This paper will focus on improving our understanding of the role of innovation and knowledge creation in the process

---

[1] The views expressed in this study are those of the author and do not necessarily reflect the views of the United Nations, its Member States, or the Institutions to which the author is affiliated.

Comments from Tanja Sinozic, University of Sussex, are gratefully acknowledged by the author.

of economic development. TNCs play a pivotal role in global knowledge creation and, although they represent a small component of the learning or innovation system, which furthers knowledge creation, they are important catalysts. It is necessary to define and explain some important underlying concepts and trends regarding knowledge creation in general, before proceeding to place these concepts in a developing country context and, to highlight the issues and opportunities that TNC-assisted knowledge creation presents.

1. Globalization, innovation and technology

Globalization is an ongoing *process*, rather than an *event*. Economic globalization implies *the growing interdependence of locations and economic units across countries and regions* (Narula 2003). The term interdependence is used very deliberately here. Cross-border linkages between economic entities do not imply globalization, merely internationalization. Trading activities do not necessarily result in interdependence. The new element of international business is the growth of FDI and the TNC. When we distinguish between trade, long-term capital flows, portfolio investment and FDI, we come to an important differentiation. Historically, international business activity used to be dominated by the development of vertical linkages, with a flow of goods between locations, in response to varying elasticities of supply and demand. Raw materials were transported from one location to another, manufactured, and transported to a third location for sale. Factors of production were immobile, and although capital did in fact get relocated, these were capital flows rather than capital embodied in physical assets or personnel and, there was no significant integration of operations in disparate locations within the control and management of the same individuals. Firms were *international*, but neither *multinational* nor *transnational*. International business and economic activity were *extensive* in the sense that the value of goods and capital exchanged were considerable, and involved numerous countries and actors, who were all dependent upon each others' patronage. But it was not *intensive*, in that activities were largely not integrated across borders.

Technological change and innovation are acknowledged almost universally as determinants of globalization. Technology implies the application of scientific knowledge for practical aims. Technology is the application of scientific concepts that help us to understand our environment, and allow us to convert this knowledge to develop and fabricate artefacts. Technology and science are *cumulative*, and build upon previous science and technology. The *practical* dividing line between science and technology is not always clear. Science and technology advance through *innovation*, which represents change in the stock of knowledge. Technology and science are subsets of knowledge. The difference is sometimes considered to be in the intent of the work, in that science is conducted in the altruistic thirst for information, while firms increase their knowledge base in order to create a product or a service. But this difference has also been blurred.

In a very general sense, innovation may mean the introduction of *any* novelty, but in economic and technology literature it has come to have a more precise meaning. An invention is an idea, sketch or model of any new or improved device, product, process or system. Innovations only occur when the new product, device or process is involved in a commercial transaction. Multiple inventions may be involved in achieving an innovation. In the Schumpeterian sense, scientific discoveries and inventions would not be termed innovation although they might fall within a second, broader, type of definition, which is concerned with the entire *process* of innovation, including antecedent work not necessarily undertaken by the entrepreneur. The broad definition of innovation as used here implies *changes in the knowledge, ability and techniques required to produce goods and services of higher or better quality per unit price,* while technology represents the cumulative stock of these innovations. It is to be emphasized that although knowledge creation and innovation are often associated with manufacture and design of new, high-technology products such as aircraft, computer components and large industrial projects, this is not always the case. Innovations can also be the discovery of a better or cheaper way to affix labels to beer bottles, a more appropriate technology to extract palm oil from palm kernels, a modified feed to improve the milk production of cows, or a superior management information system. Technology therefore – for the purposes of this paper – includes all activities that provide assets with which an economic unit can generate products or services. Science provides us with more generic knowledge, which may or may not generate products and services. As will be discussed in this paper, the challenge for many developing countries is to improve the process by which science and invention lead to innovation, thus providing a tangible economic return.

2. Knowledge creation in developing countries

Knowledge creation is often associated with formal activities within R&D that is undertaken in a systematic manner within universities and specialized public and private R&D facilities. However, these formal means represent only a small proportion of knowledge creation. Knowledge creation is a much larger and more systemic phenomenon, although formal facilities account for a large percentage of output. There are two points to be emphasized here.

- First, measuring the informal aspect of knowledge creation is immensely difficult, since its benefits and value cannot always be identified before it is used or sold. These informal aspects are also hard to benchmark, because a large proportion of them are qualitative in nature, in the form of managerial or service innovations and improvements in processes. Finding novel means to reduce the costs of pesticide use on a farm may provide cost savings of a few pennies per kilo to a small farmer, and represents the creation of new knowledge. However, it is often not possible to measure its exact value or, to determine whether this innovation is superior to a similar technique developed by another farmer in another location.

- Second, in developing countries, the informal sector tends to be very large. Developing countries undertake less than 8% of the formal R&D activities globally, and much of these tend to be undertaken by public, state-supported organizations such as universities and research institutes. It is within the domain of R&D expenditures of private enterprise in developing countries, that TNCs can play an important role, although this varies considerably by country.

In general, despite the large amounts of FDI in terms of capital values, TNCs still tend to largely concentrate their more strategic and core activities close to home. In other words, they remain more deeply embedded in their home country than elsewhere. A large proportion of even the most internationalized TNCs tend to exhibit significant inertia regarding their more strategic activities, such as R&D and headquarters functions that tend to stay at home. General Electric for instance has approximately 1,600 researchers in its United States facility, and about 400 in its two international corporate research laboratories. One point that derives indirectly from these data is that if FDI by developed country firms in other developed countries tends to have such low levels of embeddedness in locations where they have been present for many years, it is not surprising that TNCs in developing countries have an even lower level of embeddedness.

3. Foreign affiliates within host-country systems

It has been pointed out that public-sector knowledge creation is often the mainstay of R&D in developing countries, and that within the private sector, TNCs play a leading role.

However, despite the relatively large share of investment (relative to the size of the overall economy) in knowledge creation, this does not always prove to be beneficial to economic development. For developmental benefits to derive from innovation, it is essential that knowledge flows efficiently between different groups within an economy, and this is unfortunately not always the case.

Innovation involves complex interactions between a firm and its environment. The environment is not confined to the firms' networks of direct customers and suppliers only; it stretches much further. It also includes the broader factors shaping their behaviour and activities: the social and cultural context; the institutional and organizational framework; infrastructure; knowledge creating and diffusing institutions, and so on. Within a system, there exists a broad knowledge base outside industrial enterprises and, this base is central to technological accumulation by industries. Learning and innovation involve complex interactions between firms and their environment. This is the essence of the systems approach to technology.

A system, does not necessarily mean that the influences on industrial innovation are systematically organized (Narula 2003). To put it simply, a system means a regularly interacting or interdependent group forming a unified whole. A system is in most cases the serendipitous intertwining of economic actors that defines the stock of knowledge in a given location (Etzkowitz and Leydesdorff 2000). For instance, changes in the educational policies of the government are likely to affect other actors and institutions, and influence the process and extent of technological learning in the future.

Economic actors refer to two groups: The *first* group consists of firms – private and public – engaged in innovatory activity, and the *second* consists of non-firms that determine the knowledge infrastructure that supplements and supports firm-specific innovation. Knowledge infrastructure is defined in the sense proposed by Smith (1997) as being "generic, multi-user and indivisible" and consisting of public research institutes, universities, organizations for standards, intellectual property protection etc, that enables and promotes science and technology development.

In a system, the efficiency of economic actors – firm or non-firm – depends on how much and how efficiently they interact. The means by which interactions take place are referred to as institutions in the economics literature, though sociologists prefer to speak of social capital. Institutions are the "sets of common habits, routines, established practices, rules, or laws that regulate the interaction between individuals and groups" (Edquist and Johnson 1997). Institutions create the milieu within which innovation is undertaken; they establish the ground rules for interaction between economic actors and represent a sort of "culture". Institutions are associated with public sector organizations, but are not exclusively so. It is not only the creation of new knowledge but also the diffusion of extant knowledge that determine the national knowledge stock and the accumulation of national absorptive capacity.

The role of formal institutions has traditionally been considered under the rubric of political economy and has been the focus of debate on the role of the state in establishing, promoting and sustaining learning. Conventional wisdom now argues that governments are essential to promoting inter-linkages between the elements of absorptive capacity and to creating the opportunities for economic actors to absorb and internalize spillovers.

The importance of building institutions cannot be overstated: efficient institutions can contribute more to economic growth than location or trade (Rodrik et al. 2002). Institutions can be formal or informal. Formal institutions include the intellectual property regime, competition policy, technical standards, taxation, incentives for innovation, and education. Informal institutions are more difficult to define, but are associated with creating and promoting links between the various actors. For example, the government may play a role in encouraging firms to collaborate with universities or in promoting entrepreneurship.

Developing countries have switched reluctantly from inward-looking strategies with a large role for the government to market-friendly strategies that force them to face a new multilateral milieu, one in which they have little experience and with which they are often poorly prepared to cope. Institutions continue to remain largely independent and national. While formal institutions can be legislated, modifying and developing informal institutions is a complex and slow process, since they cannot be created simply by government fiat. Developed countries have taken 50 years to liberalize and adjust, but even they have faced considerable inertia. For instance, they have yet to reform their agricultural industries.

Innovation systems are built upon a relationship of trust, iteration and interaction between firms and the knowledge infrastructure, within the framework of institutions based on experience and familiarity of each other over relatively long periods of time. It is certainly true that institutions are often associated with spatial proximity (Freeman 1992). This is not unusual, given the concentration of most firms' production and R&D activities close to, or in their home location over long periods. Besides, knowledge diffuses more rapidly when actors are geographically concentrated (Ehrnberg and Jacobson 1997). This partly accounts for the tendency of firms to locate R&D (or at least the most strategically significant elements) closer to headquarters.

Nonetheless, as firms respond to demand conditions and, because there is increasing need to seek complementary assets in multi-technology, knowledge based industries, firms have spread out spatially and sought to relocate some of their activities in host locations. In engaging in foreign operation in new locations, these operations have gradually become embedded in the host environment. It is germane to this discussion to note that the routines and institutions associated with systems of production in a particular location are related but not identical to systems of innovation. That is, networks associated with production in a location are not quite the same for R&D.

In a purely domestic innovation system, comprised of purely domestic or local sources of primary knowledge (excluding the international and cross-border elements), the path of technological development is determined primarily by domestic factors. The technological development trajectory is driven largely by the changing demand of local customers. Likewise, domestic governmental organizations determine domestic industrial policy, which in turn determines domestic industrial structure. National non-firm sources of knowledge and national universities also determine the kinds of skills that engineers and scientists possess, and the kinds of technologies that these individuals have appropriate expertise in, the kinds of technologies in which basic and applied research is conducted in and thereby, the industrial specialization and competitive advantages of the firm sector.

However, few (if any) such purely national systems exist. In reality, the sources of knowledge available in a typical national system are a complex blend of domestic and foreign ones. In most countries, it is increasingly difficult to separate foreign knowledge sources from domestic ones. Although this is partly the result of globalization, it is also the result of changes in policy orientation. Some countries have voluntarily accepted the limitations of an isolationist industrial development model based on import-substitution and an inward-looking orientation, others more reluctantly, as part of World Bank instituted structural adjustment programmes.

Policies in most developing countries are oriented towards export-led growth and increased cross-border specialization and competition, and most countries are now trying to promote economic growth through FDI and international trade. This wave of liberalization is part of the new, received wisdom that is focused on tackling the deep-rooted causes that underlie market distortions.

Liberalization is an important force in economic globalization since it requires a multilateral view on hitherto domestic issues and promotes interdependence of economies. It is implicit within this view that FDI and TNC activity can be undertaken with much greater ease than previously. This view is enforced because countries have explicitly sought to encourage TNC activity as a source of much-needed capital and technology. In addition to financial crises, the general warming of attitudes towards FDI emanates from an accelerating pace of technical change and the emergence of integrated production networks of TNCs (Lall 2000).

There is a clear link between the geographical spread of the TNC and the process of technological change. Firms (of which TNCs are a subset) expand their (international) activities depending upon the strength (or weakness) of their competitive assets. These are not only confined to technological assets in the sense of ownership of plant, equipment and technical knowledge embodied in their engineers and scientists. Firms of all sizes also possess competitive advantages that derive from (a) the ability (i.e. knowledge) to create efficient internal hierarchies (or internal markets) within the boundaries of the firm and (b) from being able to efficiently utilize external markets. These ownership-specific assets are unique to each individual firm, because firms themselves consist of uniquely individual human beings. Even where two firms have the same product, one may be more profitable than the other because its managers are more efficient in utilizing its resources. Some of these are associated with the efficiency with which hierarchies are organized, and referred to as organizational innovations. Improvements in the quality of these assets leads to a greater quality per unit price. Thus they can be regarded as innovations and as part of the firm's core assets. Such assets form a necessary (and sometimes sufficient) basis for a firm to remain competitive. Such assets include *inter alia* knowledge of overseas locations, capabilities associated with organizing multi-location operations, marketing and logistics, transfer pricing, etc. The point here is that ownership-specific assets – be they technological in the narrow sense, or organizational – all share the common characteristics that they are cumulative, and evolve over time. That is, firms seek to maintain a stock of these assets, and *learn*.

4. The challenges of promoting knowledge creation in developing countries

It is relatively uncontroversial to argue that economic growth occurs due to the ability of a nation's industries to develop and sustain their competitive position, and that this requires growth of capital and labour productivity. We may further postulate that economic growth concerns not just the development of knowledge through innovation, but also the diffusion of knowledge such that it may be utilized and exploited in an efficient manner. In other words, accumulated technology is an engine of growth *only* if it can be harnessed to make the best use of available resources and therefore, must also consist of the knowledge to organize transactions efficiently, whether intra-firm, intra-industry or intra-market.

Developing countries tend to be constrained in terms of resources, at several different levels. This also limits their ability to promote knowledge creation. Some of these resource constraints are associated with attitudes and the absence of stability, trust, and transparent institutions. Others have to do with capital scarcity, the limited availability of natural or created assets, and the normal limitations that derive from a weak economy. This severely limits the opportunities to promote knowledge creation in developing countries using the policy tools that are otherwise available to developed countries. This is why TNCs provide a viable alternative that many developing countries pursue. Nonetheless, simply attracting FDI does not lead to knowledge creation. Market forces cannot substitute for the role of governments in developing and promoting a proactive industrial policy. TNCs and FDI may well lead to an increase in productivity and exports, but they do not necessarily result in increased competitiveness of the domestic sector or increased industrial capacity, which ultimately determines economic growth in the long run. FDI *per se* does not provide growth opportunities unless a domestic industrial sector exists which has the necessary technological capacity to profit from the externalities from TNC activity. This is well illustrated by the inability of many Asian countries that have relied on a passive FDI-dependent strategy to upgrade their industrial development (Lall and Narula 2004).

In many cases, foreign affiliates are so well embedded that they are regarded as part of the domestic environment. This reflects not just the length of time that these affiliates have been present (e.g. ABB in Norway), or that the affiliate is jointly owned (e.g. Hindustan Lever in India) or has been acquired (e.g. Nycomed-Amersham, Unilever, Reed Elsevier), but also the nature of the industry, and the growing trend towards consolidation in industries with low growth and opportunities of global rationalization (e.g. metals, banking, automobiles). Nonetheless, the interaction between domestic firms and foreign affiliates varies considerably, either because domestic firms are largely present in different industries or, because the two have evolved separately.

In the case of developing countries, such knowledge dependencies are often more pronounced in the case of the non-firm sector, in that universities and research organizations tend to be linked with international agencies, universities and organizations in other countries, sometimes through supranational organizations. Nonetheless, the role of TNCs remains important even in developing countries, as foreign affiliates tend to be linked with their parent corporations, as well as other affiliates in other countries. The high cost of maintaining a wide network of affiliates and the high cost of innovating, means that TNCs are always on the look-out for domestic firms in their host countries with whom they can either collaborate or from whom they can acquire important inputs for their operations. Domestic firms also seek (and are sought as) partners in international R&D consortia because there is a convergence in technological trajectories across countries, as firms seek the best partners in a given industry regardless of their national origin (Narula and Hagedoorn 1999, Narula 2003). This creates considerable potential – which may initially be modest – for smaller domestic firms and public sector organizations to benefit from the presence of TNCs, and to acquire and transfer knowledge assets. When TNCs establish affiliates in a particular location they need to build linkages with domestic agents in order to carry out their operations, and these linkages constitute one of the ways in which skills and technological transfer is thought to disseminate to the rest of the economy. Thus TNCs can promote domestic enterprise and technological learning in the entire national system, as they seek cheaper local alternatives to inputs, and can act as catalysts for system-wide learning.

It is worth pointing out that many developing countries seem prone to technological learning and attracting TNCs in "white elephant" projects, which neither fit their comparative advantage nor are the capabilities of the systems able to supply the needs of such projects. A typical example is Nigeria's investment in satellite technology. TNCs are unlikely to respond to investment opportunities that provide little or no opportunity for their own growth. *Ceteris paribus*, TNCs prefer to use technologies that are suited to their own needs, and the purposes for which they have made the investment. TNCs generally do not make available their proprietary assets available at the whims of governments; rather they tailor their investment decisions to the existing market needs and locational advantages, especially skills and capabilities in which the domestic economy has a comparative advantage (Lall 2000).

The TNC investment motive and its overall strategy are important factors to consider. For example, domestic market oriented affiliates generally purchase more locally than do export oriented firms because of lower quality requirements and technical specifications (Reuber et al 1973, Altenburg 2000). As a result, foreign affiliates are more likely to be integrated backward in the host country when they source relatively simple inputs. For example, in the case of FDI in agro-based industries, there is a greater likelihood for affiliates to be integrated backward, especially given the early stage of development of the host country. Rodriguez-Clare (1996) argues that more linkages are created when production by TNCs uses intermediate goods intensively, when communication costs between parent and affiliate are large and when the home and host markets are not too different in terms of intermediate goods produced.

Affiliates established through mergers and acquisitions are likely to have stronger links with domestic suppliers than those established through greenfield investment (UNCTAD 2000, Scott-Kennel and Enderwick 2001), since such FDI can find established linkages upon acquisition that are likely to be retained if they are efficient. Most importantly, linkages vary by industry. In the primary sector, the scope for location-specific vertical linkages is often limited, due to the production processes and capital intensity of such operations. In manufacturing, the potential for vertical linkages is broader, depending on the extent of intermediate inputs to total production and the type of production processes (Lall 1980). Blomström and Kokko (1997) suggest that "some of the host country characteristics that may influence the extent of linkages

– and thereby in the longer term the extent of spillovers – are market size, local content regulations and the size and technological capability of local firms". They argue that there is a propensity for linkages to increase over time, as the skill level of local entrepreneurs grows, new suppliers emerge and local content increases. The time factor is highlighted also by Rasiah (1994) and is related to the experience and integration of a foreign affiliate in the host country through greater indigenization of operations in terms of management, knowledge about their location and operations. The embeddedness of firms is often (but not always) a function of how long the TNCs have been present in the host country, since firms tend to build incrementally.

Technology diffusion through backward linkages presupposes that first, domestic firms in the industry exist, and second, they possess the capacity to usefully internalize the knowledge being made available by the TNC. Diffusion to the rest of the economy may not occur because of deficiencies in the institutional capability systems of the host country or other deficiencies in the absorptive capacity of domestic economic agents in the host country. Wider technology gaps between domestic firms and foreign affiliates are more likely to result in fewer backward linkages as well as the type of technological content of inputs sourced locally (Narula and Portelli forthcoming).

It is obvious that national governments have a strong interest in the ability of firms in a given location to conduct competitiveness-enhancing activities, and particularly those associated with the creation and deployment of knowledge capital. These reasons can be qualified under two main headings, *viz.* the promotion of the wealth creating assets of its firms and, maintaining and improving indigenous resources and capabilities. By doing so, it can help to maintain and improve its own locational attractiveness to mobile and footloose investors (of whatever nationality) to conduct high value adding activities. These two issues are strongly related, since the presence of highly competitive firms at a given location acts as a location advantage, often prompting a virtuous circle. Conversely, strong location advantages, such as the presence of support institutions and firms, infrastructure and skilled manpower will enhance the ownership advantages of firms located there.

The role of governments in improving the quality of human capital cannot be over-emphasized. One of the primary determinants behind technological accumulation and absorptive capacity is human capital. Qualified human resources are essential in monitoring the evolution of external knowledge and in evaluating their relevance and, for the integration of these technologies into productive activities. Human capital represents an important subset of absorptive capabilities, and this is well acknowledged by policy makers everywhere. However, the presence of a highly skilled labour force is a necessary condition. Simply providing tertiary level education and skilled manpower does not lead to increased R&D, nor is there a direct connexion between education and technological competence. The availability of a large stock of suitably qualified workers does not in itself result in efficient absorption of knowledge, as is well illustrated by the former centrally planned economies of Eastern Europe. But the quality of the training and the ability of industry to exploit available skills in R&D or other technical effort matter a great deal.

5. Conclusion

The failure of most countries to successfully promote knowledge creation and take advantage of TNC-assisted knowledge creation reflects two difficulties. The first is the difficulty to integrate various policies in a systemic way; the second is the difficulty of transforming institutions associated with the old order of import substitution. Policies, administrators and policy-makers have largely attempted to graft the new model onto the remnants of the old model, partly because political and social interest groups are resistant to change, and partly because rapid and sweeping policy shifts require considerable time for the informal institutions to adjust (Lall and Narula 2004).

References

Altenburg T (2000). "Linkages and spillovers between transnational corporations and small and medium-sized enterprises in developing countries: opportunities and best policies". In UNCTAD, ed., *TNC-SME Linkages for Development: Issues-Experiences-Best Practices.* New York and Geneva: United Nations, United Nations document UNCTAD/ITE/TEB1: 3-61.

Benito G, Grogaard B and Narula R (2003). "Environmental influences on MNE subsidiary roles: economic integration and the Nordic countries", *Journal of International Business Studies,* 34: 443-456.

Blomström M and Kokko A (1997). "How foreign investment affects host countries". *Policy Research Working Paper.* Washington D.C.: World Bank.

Edquist C and Johnson B (1997). "Institutions and organisations in systems of innovation". In Edquist C, ed., *Systems of Innovation: Technologies, Institutions and Organisations.* London and Washington: Pinter.

Ehrnberg E and Jacobsson S (1997). "Technological discontinuities and incumbents' performance: an analytical framework". In Edquist C, ed., *Systems of Innovation: Technologies, Institutions and Organisations.* London and Washington: Pinter.

Etzkowitz H and Leydesdorff L (2000). "The dynamics of innovation: from national systems and "Mode 2" to a triple helix of university-industry-government relations", *Research Policy* 29(2): 109-123.

Lall S (1980). "Vertical inter-firm linkages in LDCs: an empirical study, *Oxford Bulletin of Economics and Statistics* 42(3): 209-222.

_____ (2000). "Transnational corporations and technology flows". In D Nayyar, ed., *New Roles and Functions for the United Nations and Bretton Woods Institutions*. Helsinki: United Nations University WIDER.

_____ and Narula R (2004). "FDI and its role in economic development: Do we need a new agenda?", *European Journal of Development Research* 16: 447 - 464.

Narula R (2003). *Globalisation and Technology*. Cambridge: Polity Press.

_____ and Portelli B (forthcoming). "Foreign direct investment through acquisitions and implications for technological upgrading: case evidence from Tanzania", *European Journal of Development Research* 18, forthcoming.

Rasiah R (1994). "Flexible production systems and local machine tool subcontracting: electronics component multinationals in Malaysia, *Cambridge Journal of Economics* 18: 279-298.

Reuber GL, Crookell H, Emerson M and Gallais-Hamonno G (1973). *Private Foreign Investment in Development*. Oxford: Clarendon Press.

Rodriguez-Clare A (1996). "Multinationals, linkages, and economic development", *American Economic Review* 85: 852-873.

Rodrik D, Subramanian A and Trebbi A (2002). "Institutions rule: the primacy of institutions over geography and integration in economic development". *NBER Working Paper* 9305.

Scott-Kennel J and Enderwick P (2001). "The degree of linkage of foreign direct investment in New Zealand industry". Victoria University of Wellington, Wellington. Mimeo.

UNCTAD (2000). *World Investment Report 2000: Cross-Border Mergers and Acquisitions and Development*. New York and Geneva: United Nations. United Nations publication, Sales No. E.00.II.D.20.

The complexity and internationalization of innovation: the root causes

Dieter Ernst[1]

The internationalization of innovation continues to lag behind the internationalization of finance, distribution and manufacturing but, it is now experiencing a rapid proliferation. The main drivers are TNCs who are increasing their overseas investment in R&D, while seeking to integrate geographically dispersed innovation clusters into global networks of production, engineering, development and research. This adds an important new dimension to the evolution of cross-border corporate networks. Global innovation networks are now being crafted, in addition to the existing global production networks.

Since the late 1990s, this process has no longer been restricted to the industrial heartlands of the OECD. The internationalization of innovation is now expanding into new locations in emerging economies, primarily in South, East and South-East Asia. Going beyond adaptation, R&D in the new locations now also encompasses the creation of new products and processes. TNCs are at the forefront of these developments, experimenting with new approaches to the management of global innovation networks. However, local firms are playing an increasingly active role as sources of innovation and in shaping relevant standards.

As R&D and innovation are critical for economic growth, competitiveness and welfare, the internationalization of innovation creates new challenges and opportunities for a wide range of public policies that affect FDI and economic development. In the home countries of TNCs that are internationalizing R&D and innovation, there are concerns that

---

[1] The views expressed in this study are those of the author and do not necessarily reflect the views of the United Nations, its Member States, or the Institutions to which the author is affiliated.

this may extend the "hollowing-out" of their economies well beyond manufacturing to research and development, the most fundamental sources of their economic growth.[2] These fears may feed into protectionism (Granstrand and Sjölander 1990). On the other hand, emerging economies (the host countries of international R&D and innovation) are all searching for strategies that would enable them to benefit from integration into global R&D and innovation networks. Prominent examples are attempts by governments and domestic firms in East and South-East Asia's leading electronics exporting economies (China, the Republic of Korea, Taiwan Province of China, Singapore and Malaysia) to build innovative capabilities within the above global networks.

Research on the internationalization of innovation has recently received a boost, but it is still at a very early stage. There are few robust data on the drivers and especially the impacts of these processes. There are now concerted efforts to close this research gap for the internationalization of innovation among industrialized countries. However, there is limited research on what precisely is driving the more recent extension of R&D and innovation into new locations outside the established centres of excellence in the United States, Japan and Europe. Even less is known about possible impacts, and effective policy responses.

This paper addresses a particularly important unresolved question: *What explains the internationalization of innovative activities that involve highly complex technological knowledge?* In innovation theory, it is assumed that complexity constrains the internationalization of innovation. This is based on the proposition that physical proximity is advantageous for innovative activities that involve highly complex technological knowledge. In a frequently quoted article, the late Keith Pavitt and his co-author Pari Patel (Pavitt and Patel 1991) used patent

---

[2] See for instance, Friedman 2005.

data to demonstrate that innovative activities of the world's largest TNCs were among the least internationalized of their functions. They argued that firms tended to concentrate innovation in their home countries, in order to facilitate the exchange of complex knowledge. Hence, complexity explained why innovation remained an important case of "non-globalization".

However, chip design, a process that creates the high value in the IT industry and that requires complex knowledge, does not confirm this proposition. Over the past few years, a heavy concentration in a few centres of excellence (mainly in the United States, but also in Europe and Japan), has given way to growing organizational and geographical mobility. Vertical specialization within global design networks represents an important test case for the study of global innovation networks. Global design networks are shaped by the progressive *dis-integration* of the design value chain and to its *geographical dispersion*. Vertical specialization within global design networks thus combines the "outsourcing" of stages of chip design to specialized suppliers and its "offshoring" across national boundaries. Of particular importance has been a rapid expansion of chip design in leading Asian electronics exporting countries that has been accompanied by substantial progress in the complexity of design.

1. Spatial stickiness of innovation

For decades, the dominant position of researchers has been that innovation, in contrast to most other stages of the value chain, is highly immobile. Cognitive complexity is the main reason for such spatial stickiness of innovation. It is assumed in innovation theory that to cope with the demanding requirements of cognitive complexity, firms have a strong incentive to concentrate innovation in their home countries. However, recent empirical research on globalization has clearly established that the centre of gravity has shifted beyond the national economy. International linkages proliferate, as markets for capital, goods, services, knowledge and labour are integrated across borders. While integration is far from perfect in markets for technology (Arora et al. 2001), it is nevertheless transforming the geography of innovation (Ernst 2002a). This process is well captured in Cantwell's important observation that instead of a few pre-eminent centres of innovation, there are now "multiple locations for innovation, and even lower-order or less developed centres can still be sources of innovation." (Cantwell 1995: 172).[3]

2. Root causes of organizational and geographical mobility

To explain the internationalization of innovation, this section highlights the following four general root causes that are gradually reducing the constraints imposed by knowledge complexity on the organizational and geographical mobility of innovation (Ernst 2003a):

- institutional change through liberalization;
- the impact of general-purpose technologies (such as ICT);
- transformations in markets, competition and industrial organization (especially vertical specialization through network arrangements);

---

[3] A particularly intriguing example is China's pioneering role in the development of the world's first commercially operated nuclear "pebble bed" reactor that offers the hope of cheap, safe and easily expandable nuclear power stations (China in drive for nuclear reactors, *Financial Times*, 8 February 2005: 4). Within Asia, new innovation clusters have also emerged for broadband technology and applications in the Republic of Korea and Singapore, for digital consumer devices in the Republic of Korea, China, Hong Kong (China) and Taiwan Province of China, and for software engineering and project management in India. Other examples are Europe's newly emerging innovation clusters for microelectronics technology in Crolles (near Grenoble), at the Inter-University Microelectronics Center (IMEC) at Leuven, Belgium and in Dresden, Germany.

- adjustments in corporate strategy and business models.

a. Liberalization

Liberalization has four main elements: trade liberalization; liberalization of capital flows; liberalization of FDI policies; and privatization. While each of these has generated separate debates in the literature, they hang together. Earlier success in trade liberalization has sparked an expansion of trade and FDI, increasing the demand for cross-border capital flows. This has increased the pressure for liberalization of capital markets, forcing more and more countries to open their capital accounts. In turn this has led to a liberalization of FDI policies, and to "privatization tournaments".

The overall effect of liberalization has been a considerable reduction in the cost and risks of international transactions and a massive increase in international liquidity. TNCs have been the primary beneficiaries: liberalization provides them with a greater range of choices for market entry between trade, licensing, subcontracting, and franchising (*locational specialization*); it provides better access to external resources and capabilities that a TNC needs to complement its core competencies (*outsourcing*); and it has reduced the constraints for a geographic dispersion of the value chain (*spatial mobility*). During the last part of the 20th century, this has given rise to the spread of global production networks. Since the turn of the century, TNC-cantered network arrangements are now also encompassing innovation, giving rise to global innovation networks.

b. Information and communication technology

The second important root cause of the increasing mobility of innovation is the rapid development and diffusion of ICT. ICT has had a dual impact: it has increased the need for, and has created, new opportunities for globalization. The *cost* and *risk* of developing ICT has been a primary cause for *market* globalization: international markets are required to amortize fully the enormous R&D expenses associated with rapidly evolving process and product ICT (Kobrin 1997: 149). Of equal importance are the huge expenses for ICT-based information management (Brynjolfsson and Hitt 2000). As the extent of a company's R&D effort is determined by the nature of its technology and competition rather than its size, this rapid growth of R&D spending requires a corresponding expansion of sales, if profitability is to be maintained. No national market, not even the United States market, is large enough to amortize such huge expenses.

ICT-based information management also creates new opportunities for globalization, enabling international production rather than exports to become the main vehicle for international market share expansion. Over time, the expansion of global production networks requires the parallel extension of engineering support services. This implies that knowledge diffusion among different network nodes becomes the necessary glue that enables global production networks to grow. At some stage, once an individual global production network node has reached a critical threshold, TNCs may need to upgrade these activities to include product development and design. Much depends of course on the development of local innovation capabilities and systems (Ernst and Kim 2002).

Of critical importance has been the enabling role played by ICT: these general-purpose technologies (Lipsey and Carlaw forthcoming) have substantially increased the mobility, i.e. *dispersion* of firm-specific resources and capabilities across national boundaries; they also provide much greater scope for cross-border linkages, i.e. the *integration* of dispersed specialized clusters. This has substantially reduced the friction of time and space, not only for sales and production, but also for R&D and other innovative activities. A TNC can now serve distant markets equally as well as local producers; it can also now disperse more and more stages of its value chain across national borders in order to select the most cost-effective location.

In addition, ICT and related organizational innovations provide effective mechanisms for constructing flexible infrastructures that can link together and coordinate economic transactions at distant locations (Antonelli 1992, Hagstrøm 2000). This has important implications for organizational choices and locational strategies of firms. In essence, ICT fosters the development of leaner, meaner and more agile production and innovation systems that cut across firm boundaries and national borders. The underlying vision is that of a network of firms that enable a TNC to respond quickly to changing circumstances, even if much of its value chain has been dispersed.

c. Transformations in markets, competition and industrial organization

The third root cause of the increasing organizational and geographical mobility of innovation is found in the transformations in markets, competition and industrial organization that result from the interplay of liberalization and ICT. "Globalization" is a widely used shorthand for transformations in markets, defined as the integration, across borders, of markets for capital, goods, services, knowledge, and labour (Ernst 2005b). Barriers to integration continue to exist in each of these different markets (especially for low-wage labour), so integration is far from perfect but, there is no doubt that a massive integration of markets has taken place across borders that, only a short while ago, seemed to be impenetrable.

This has drastically changed the dynamics of competition. The geographic scope of competition has broadened and competitive requirements are now much more complex. Competition now cuts across national borders - a firm's position in one country is no longer independent from its position in other countries (Porter 1990). The firm must be present in all major growth markets (*dispersion*). It must also integrate its activities on a worldwide scale, in order to exploit and coordinate linkages between these different locations (*integration*). Competition also cuts across industry boundaries and market segments: mutual raiding of established market segment fiefdoms has become the norm, making it more difficult for firms to identify market niches and to grow with them.

This growing complexity of competition has changed the determinants of location, as well as industrial and firm organization. In the case of location decisions, while both market access and cost reductions remain important, it has become clear that they have to be reconciled with a number of equally important requirements that encompass:

- the exploitation of uncertainty through improved operational flexibility (Kogut 1985, Kogut and Kulatilaka 1994);
- a compression of speed-to-market through reduced product development and product life cycles (Flaherty 1986);
- learning and the acquisition of specialized external capabilities through asset-augmenting R&D (Hedlund 1986, Kogut 1989, Kogut and Zander 1993, Dunning 1998, Zander and Kogut 1995, Kuemmerle 1996, Patel and Vega, 1999, Le Bas and Sierra 2002);
- the need to access the evolving global talent pool (D'Costa 2004, Ernst, 2005a) and, a shift of market penetration strategies from established to new and unknown markets (Christensen 1997).

As TNCs seek to cope with the increasingly demanding determinants of location, this induces them to consider the offshoring of gradually more knowledge-intensive activities, including some aspects of product development. In this sense, it is possible to argue that the transition from the offshoring of manufacturing to the "outsourcing of innovation" (*Business Week* 21 March 2005) is an evolutionary process and, that TNCs are gradually building global innovation networks onto their existing global production networks.

Changes in industrial organization are equally important. No firm, not even a dominant market leader, can generate internally all the different capabilities that are necessary to cope with the requirements of global competition. Thus, competitive success critically depends on "vertical specialization": TNCs selectively "outsource" certain capabilities from specialized suppliers, and they "offshore" them to new, lower-cost locations. While vertical specialization initially was focused on final assembly and lower-end component manufacturing, it is increasingly being pushed into higher-end value chain stages, including product development and design capabilities. To make this happen, TNCs had to shift from individual to increasingly collective forms of organization, from the multidivisional (M-form) functional hierarchy (Williamson 1975 and 1985, Chandler 1977) to the networked global flagship model (Ernst, 2002b).

The electronics industry has become an important breeding ground for this new industrial organization model. A massive process of vertical specialization has segmented an erstwhile vertically integrated industry into closely interacting horizontal layers (Grove 1996). Until the early 1980s, IBM personified 'vertical integration': almost all ingredients necessary to design, produce and commercialize computers remained internal to the firm. This was true for semiconductors, hardware, operating systems, application software, and sales and distribution.

Since then, vertical specialization became the industry's defining feature (Ernst 2003a). Most activities that used to characterize a computer company are now being farmed out to multiple layers of specialized suppliers, giving rise to rapid market segmentation and, an ever finer specialization within each of the above value chain stages. Over time, as firms have accumulated experience in managing global distribution and production networks and, as they are learning from successes and failures in inter-firm collaboration, this has given rise to new and increasingly sophisticated forms of corporate network arrangements. It is on the basis of such learning processes that TNCs are now pushing vertical specialization deeper into the innovation value chain, gradually constructing global innovation networks.

d. Adjustments in corporate strategy and business models

Vertical specialization went hand in hand with adjustments in corporate strategy and business models that further enhanced the organizational and geographical mobility of innovation. In the IT industry for instance, these adjustments were especially important in the choice of product and process specialization, in investment funding and, in human resources management. Feeding into each other, these adjustments are "systemic" in that small changes in any of them require adjustments in all the other aspects of the business model.

The spread of venture capital and related regulatory changes in the financial industry[4] have drastically changed corporate strategies of investment funding. United States venture capital firms provide access to a massive infusion of capital from United States pension funds as well as hands-on industrial expertise. As a result, start-up companies in the IT

---

[4] Important complementary changes in United States financial institutions include the launching of NASDAQ in 1971 (making it much easier for start-up firms to go public), the reduction of the capital gains tax by the United States Congress in 1978, from 49% to 28%, and, the Department of Labor decree in 1979 that pension fund money can be invested not only in listed stocks and high-grade bonds but also in more speculative assets, including new ventures (Lazonick 2005: 23).

industry now were able to raise capital for high-risk innovation projects. At the same time, global IT industry leaders have increasingly used stock to attract and retain global talent and to acquire innovative start-up companies (Lazonick 2003). Both changes in investment funding have led to far-reaching changes in corporate governance, with the result that investment decisions are now primarily oriented towards servicing shareholder requirements. This has drastically changed the parameters for innovation management. As IT firms can rely more and more on stock and venture capital, they are under increasing pressure to raise the productivity of their innovation efforts and, to commercialize as fast as possible the resulting IPRs.

As for the management of labour, the IT industry has seen a dramatically diminished commitment to long-term employment "on both sides of the employment relation" (Lazonick 2005:2), giving rise to a substantial increase in the inter-firm and geographical mobility of labour, especially for highly skilled engineers, scientists and managers. In the United States, the emergence of a "high-velocity labour market" (Hyde 2003) for IT skills is driven by the proliferation of start-up companies; a drastic increase in the recruitment of highly educated foreigners; and the spread of lavish incentives (such as stock options) to induce job-hopping.

This has raised the cost of employing IT workers in the United States. For instance, between 1993 and 1999, computer scientists and mathematicians experienced the highest salary growth (37%) of all United States occupations (NSF 2004, chapter 3, page 14). Average real annual earnings of full-time employees in California's software industry rose from $80,000 in 1994 to $180,000 in 2000, only to fall drastically to below $100,000 in 2002, after the bursting of the "New Economy" bubble. However, even in the midst of the IT industry recession, employees in the United States IT industry continued to earn, on average, much more than in most other industries of the economy and, between five and ten times more than their counterparts in Asia (outside of Japan). In 2002, the average annual wage in the United States IT industry was $67,440 (with a high of $99,440 in the software industry), compared with $36,250 in all private-sector industries (United States, Department of Commerce 2003, appendix table 2.3). This has created a powerful catalyst for IT firms in the United States to increase their overseas investment in R&D, in order to tap into the growing pool of educated and experienced IT talent that is available in Asia at much lower wages.

3. Changes in innovation management

The above transformations in markets, technology, competition and strategy have provoked fundamental changes in innovation management, further enhancing the mobility of innovation. A transition is under way towards gradually more open corporate innovation systems, based on an increasing vertical specialization of innovation. What explains the dynamics of these changes, and how do they shape the internationalization of innovation? This section highlights a gradual opening and networking of corporate innovation systems; examines the role played by evolving global markets for technology and for knowledge workers in the transition to global corporate innovation networks; and finally, discusses possible strategic benefits for TNCs.

a. Opening and networking of corporate innovation systems

Corporate innovation management needs to address four tasks simultaneously: to develop innovative capabilities (including R&D);[5] to recruit and retain educated and

---

[5] "Innovative capabilities" are defined as the skills, knowledge and management techniques needed to design, produce, improve and commercialize "artefacts", i.e. products, services, machinery and processes (Ernst 2005c).

experienced knowledge workers; to develop and adjust innovation process management (methodologies, organization and routines) in order to improve efficiency and time-to-market; and to match all three tasks with the corporation's business model, which determines customers, market segments, pricing, the degree of in-sourcing and outsourcing and, which defines the structure of required distribution, production and innovation networks. All four tasks are intrinsically interdependent but, of greatest importance is compliance with the firm's business model. In fact, if a firm pursues the first three tasks without a clear definition of the business model, this is likely to produce commercial failure.

The growing organizational and geographical mobility of innovation creates new challenges, but also provides new opportunities for innovation management. The challenge is that no firm, not even a global market leader like IBM, can mobilize all the diverse resources, capabilities and bodies of knowledge internally. Instead, both the sources and the use of knowledge become increasingly externalized. Now, firms must supplement the in-house creation of new knowledge and capabilities with external knowledge sourcing strategies. There are strong pressures to reduce in-house basic and applied research and, to focus primarily on product development and the absorption of external knowledge (e.g. Chesbrough 2003, Arora et al. 2001). No longer does this externalization of innovation stop at the national border. Firms increasingly need to tap sources of knowledge that are located overseas (Ernst 2002a).

At the same time, corporate innovation management is under increasing pressure to commercialize existing intellectual property rights through aggressive technology licensing. Furthermore, recruitment of knowledge workers now draws on an evolving global labour market, especially for scarce bottleneck skills, in order to keep a cap on rising costs of R&D and engineering. Finally, a corporation's business model is no longer exclusively shaped by peculiar characteristics of home country markets, but needs to adjust to diverse idiosyncratic overseas markets.

The result has been a gradual opening and networking of corporate innovation systems (Arora et al. 2001, Chesbrough 2003, Ernst, 2005b). For instance, the *Science and Engineering Indicators 2004* report by the United States NSF highlights the increasing importance of innovation networks that cut across industries and national borders. The report argues that "the speed, complexity, and multidisciplinary nature of scientific research, coupled with the increased relevance of science and the demands of a globally competitive environment, have ... encouraged an innovation system increasingly characterized by networking and feedback among R&D performers, technology users and their suppliers and, across industries and national boundaries" (United States NSF 2004, Volume I, page IV-36).

Chesbrough's concept of "open innovation" provides a useful stylized model of this gradual opening of corporate innovation systems. However, the model does not address explicitly the international dimension, i.e. the development of global innovation networks. In Chesbrough's model, a corporation has a "closed" innovation system, when it seeks to discover new breakthroughs, to develop them into products, to build the products in its factories and, to distribute, finance and service those products; "all within the four walls of the company" (Chesbrough 2003: 4).[6] An "open" innovation system, on the other hand, requires that the corporation redefine its business model to commercialize technologies that it has at

---

[6] Naturally, hardly any company has ever relied on a completely closed, self-contained innovation system, except in times of war or in dictatorial societies. Chesbrough's concept of a "closed innovation system" highlights two stylized organizational routines that over time constrain the economic benefits from innovation: First, the firm creates ideas for the sole purpose of using them, and second, the firm only uses ideas that have been created internally, the so-called NIH ("not invented here") syndrome (Chesbrough 2003: 29).

its disposal, both from external sources and through in-house development.

b. Global markets for technology

In an open innovation system, both the source and the use of knowledge can be external for the TNC. The firm can create ideas for external and internal use, and it can access ideas from the outside as well as from within. Firms are able to move to an open innovation system, because an increasing mobility of knowledge has created an abundance of knowledge outside the firm. "The proliferation of public scientific databases and online journals and articles, combined with low-cost internet access and high transmission rates...[provide]...access to a wealth of knowledge that was far more expensive and time-consuming to reach as recently as the early 1990s" (Chesbrough 2003: 44).

Arora et al. (2001) demonstrate that the gradual opening of corporate innovation systems is driven by the increasing division of labour in innovation.[7] This gives rise to the growth of "markets for technology", which is further enhancing the mobility of innovation. Markets for technology affect corporate innovation strategy in multiple ways, creating more space for a gradual opening and networking of corporate innovation systems. TNCs can now outsource knowledge that they need to complement their internally generated knowledge and, they can choose to license their technology, and hence enhance the rents from innovation.

The idea of knowledge outsourcing runs counter to established wisdom in innovation theory. Barney (1991) for

---

[7] The argument that technology and innovation can be the subject of a division of labour goes back to Stigler (1951). That widely quoted article argues that as the extent of the market is increasing, the division of labour would also embrace innovation, leading to the rise of stand-alone R&D laboratories that would sell their research results to other parties.

instance, argues that for a firm to grow, it must control resources that are valuable, rare and imperfectly mobile. The underlying assumption is that technological assets cannot be directly bought and sold, and the services of such assets cannot be rented. Teece (1986) demonstrates that in the absence of technology markets, firms must invest in creating "co-specialized assets" (such as the production of core components and accumulated knowledge of customer requirements) to maximize their returns from innovation. And Edith Penrose, in her pioneering study ("The theory of the growth of the firm"), concludes that "... a firm's rate of growth is limited by the growth of knowledge within it" (Penrose [1959] 1995: XVI-XVII), emphasizing the capacity for knowledge integration.

However, markets for technology broaden the choices available to a firm. There is now much greater scope for external technology sourcing. Markets for technology actually increase the penalty for the NIH ("not invented here") syndrome, i.e. a reluctance to use external technologies. As the mobility of knowledge increases, a firm's competitive success critically depends on its ability to monitor and quickly seize external sources of knowledge (Iansiti 1997). As demonstrated by Iansiti and West (1997), a company can leverage basic or generic technologies developed elsewhere, which allows it to focus on developing unique applications that better suit the needs of specific overseas markets. Industry leaders can now attempt to balance in-house innovation and external knowledge sourcing. However, external knowledge sourcing can also provide a short cut for late entrants from developing countries. For instance, companies that trail behind industry leaders in their in-house technological capabilities can now use external technology sourcing to enhance their in-house innovative capabilities (Ernst 1997 and 2000).

Markets for technology also create new opportunities for appropriating innovation rents through technology licensing. The underlying assumption is that once markets for technology exist, knowledge will be sufficiently codified and IPRs will be well defined and protected (Kogut and Zander 1993) but, theory also shows that an excessive reliance on technology licensing may be risky, as it cuts the company off from vital system integration knowledge that is necessary for continuous innovation (Grindley and Teece 1997).

c. Evolving global markets for knowledge workers[8]

Equally important for the gradual opening of corporate innovation systems has been the increasing availability of knowledge workers outside the dominant corporations and their rapidly increasing geographical mobility, first within the United States (e.g. the GI bill after World War II), then in Europe (Marshall aid for reconstruction and later various rounds of EU enlargement) and Japan and, after 1970, in the newly industrializing economies of East and South-East Asia. In all of these regions, as well as in China, India, Brazil and the Russian Federation, government policies to improve education and training, and to enhance their interaction with business needs, have helped to increase the supply of knowledge workers.

The result is an evolving global market for knowledge workers. According to the United States NSF (2004, Volume 1, chapter 3), more and more governments are implementing aggressive policies designed to attract highly trained and experienced engineers, scientists and R&D managers from abroad. TNCs are responding to the intensifying competition for scarce global talent, "by opening high-technology operations in foreign locations, developing strategic international alliances, and consummating cross-national spinoffs and mergers" (*ibid*: 0-3). For some bottleneck skills, like experienced design engineers for analogue integrated circuits, this may lead to global "auction markets" for knowledge workers, enabling them to sell their talents to the highest bidder. Overall however, the

---

[8] This section draws on Ernst 2005a.

emergence of a global market for knowledge workers seems to have kept a tight cap on increases in remuneration (Lazonick 2005). In summary, the leading TNCs can tap into global markets for knowledge workers who are readily available for hire and need not require extensive internal training or the inducement of lifelong employment.

Until the turn of the century, the United States was the main beneficiary of the globalization of knowledge workers, as the main recipient of a global brain drain. A 1998 NSF study showed that over 50% of the post-doctoral students at MIT and Stanford were not United States citizens, and that more than 30% of computer professionals in Silicon Valley were born outside the United States (United States NSF 2004). Data from the most recent 2000 United States Census show that in science and engineering occupations approximately 17% of bachelor's degree holders, 29% of master's degree holders, and 38% of doctorate holders were foreign born. This has enabled start-up companies to pursue "learning-by hiring away" strategies. They could rapidly ramp up complex innovation projects with highly experienced personnel that were trained by other corporations or countries. However, the main beneficiaries were major TNCs who were able to reduce the cost of research, product development and engineering by shifting from national to global recruitment strategies.

It is important to emphasize that over the last few years, the privileged position of the United States in global markets for knowledge workers, has faced new challenges. In fact, the two main concerns of the most recent Nation Science Board report on "Science & Engineering Indicators", are competing recruitment practices of foreign governments and TNCs and whether "post 9/11" visa restrictions to foreign students, scholars and engineers will dry up the erstwhile readily available supply of top talent for United States firms.

d. Strategic benefits for TNCs

An important strategic benefit that TNCs can draw from the opening and networking of corporate innovation systems is that this may facilitate the matching of business models and technology road maps. For instance, external and international knowledge sourcing can help to fill the gaps between both, at least temporarily. It can also help to identify and address "blind spots" that have gone undetected within a closed innovation system. This is of critical importance, as the increasing complexity of technology road maps poses a serious challenge to corporate innovation management.

The *International Roadmap for Semiconductors*, was co-published by the semiconductor industry associations of the United States and other leading semiconductor exporting countries (ITRS 2004). Until the mid-1990s, its primary concern was to coordinate requirements *within* fabrication that needed to be fulfilled to extend Moore's Law.[9] The road map thus focused on defining interfaces between a variety of complementary semiconductor manufacturing technologies, including photolithography (the process of using light to etch a circuit pattern on a chip), the mask (the device that contains the circuit pattern), the chemical agents used to impart the pattern, the physical size of the wafers used to hold the etched pattern and, the equipment used to measure these tiny distances reliably and accurately. For each of these different innovation agents, the road map defined the sequencing of complementary innovations, so that these technologies are produced right at the time when other required technologies will also be available, instead of being delivered too early or too late. Today, the semiconductor road map is substantially more complex, and needs to coordinate multiple interfaces between the design, fabrication and application of semiconductor devices that

---

[9] In 1965, Gordon Moore, one of the co-founders of Intel, predicted that economical integrated circuit density would double roughly every one to two years (Moore 1965).

increasingly integrate systems on a chip. Hence, it becomes much more difficult to match technology road maps and business plans. This has given rise to a progressive vertical specialization of innovation within global design networks.

Furthermore, an open corporate innovation system can help the company to hedge against failures of internal R&D projects or against slippage in capacity expansion. It also helps TNCs to multiply opportunities for technology diversification. In other words, there is a choice between "build-or-buy" new business lines. It may also accelerate the speed of the innovation cycle and reduce the very high fixed cost of investing in internal R&D capabilities.

In essence, the transition to more open innovation systems through global innovation networks reflects the recognition by incumbent market leaders that there is simply no way to prevent knowledge diffusion. Even the most aggressive attempts to slow down such diffusion (such as "black-boxing" of technology)[10] are unlikely to succeed (Ernst 2004). This explains why incumbent market leaders now prefer to exploit the diffusion of knowledge, rather than fighting rearguard battles to protect themselves against knowledge leakage.

Finally, it is important to emphasize that once a TNC relies on global innovation networks, internal R&D becomes even more important than it used to be in a "closed" innovation system. However, the internal research team now needs to develop extensive linkages with outside and especially international knowledge sources. This explains the drastic changes in the organization, routines and incentives of

---

[10] "Black box" technologies are defined as technologies "that cannot be easily imitated by competitors because they are: (1) protected under intellectual property rights, such as patents, (2) made of complex materials, processes, and know-how that cannot be copied, or (3) made using unique production methods, systems or control technologies" (Ernst 2005c).

corporate innovation management that this section has documented.

In sum, "vertical specialization" is no longer restricted to the production of goods and services, but now extends to all stages of the value chain, including research and new product development. Over the years, this process has taken on an increasingly international dimension, with the result that corporate innovation management can now "integrate distinctive knowledge from around the world as effectively as global supply chains integrate far-flung sources of raw materials, labour, components and services" (Santos, Doz and Williamson 2004: 31). Most importantly, TNCs now can proceed to construct international innovation networks that improve the productivity of R&D "by accessing knowledge from non-traditional cheaper locations" (*ibid*).

As the number of specialized suppliers of innovation modules increases, this provides a powerful boost to the organizational and geographical mobility of innovation. TNCs are now seeking to integrate geographically dispersed innovation clusters into global networks of production, engineering, development and research. Since the turn of the century, these networks have been extended to emerging new innovation clusters, especially in Asia. This is expected to provide TNCs with a new source of competitive advantage: more higher-value innovation at lower cost.

4. Conclusion

An important lesson from this analysis is that the internationalization of innovation, and its vertical specialization within global innovation networks, is driven by a combination of pull, push and enabling factors that are systemic. For host country policies, this implies that a narrow focus on demand- or supply-oriented forces can attract foreign R&D only if these policies are based on a profound understanding of the underlying changes in the methodology and organization of the relevant innovation processes in the particular industry. Only when pull, push and enabling factors are coming together, creating a virtuous circle, will host country policies attract R&D by TNCs and produce the expected results.

Another corollary of the analysis above is the critical importance of the absorptive capacity of local firms, i.e. their resources, capabilities and motivations. To stay on the global innovation networks, local firms need to invest constantly in their skills and knowledge bases. Policies to strengthen the innovative capabilities of local firms are equally important. To reap the benefits of integration into global innovation networks requires an active involvement of local, regional, and central government agencies, as well as a variety of intermediate institutions. This involvement has to take on a very different form from earlier top-down "command economy" type industrial policies.

As an immediate policy instrument, it may be necessary to import missing critical skills from overseas. This could help to catalyze necessary reforms in the domestic innovation system. But most important are support policies for local firms through local supplier development, (co-funded) skill development, standards setting, policies on IPRs and the provision of investment and innovation finance through a variety of sources, including venture capital, and initial public offerings.[11]

---

[11] An initial public offering is the first sale of stock by a private company to the public. Smaller, younger companies seeking capital to expand their businesses are the most frequent users of initial public offerings.

References

Antonelli C, ed. (1992). *The Economics of Information Networks.* Amsterdam: Elsevier North Holland.

Arora, A, Fosfuri A and Gambardella A (2001). *Markets for Technology: The Economics of Innovation and Corporate Strategy*: Cambridge, MA: MIT Press.

Barney JB (1991). "Firms' resources and sustained competitive advantage", *Journal of Management* 17: 99-120.

Brynjolfson E and Hitt LM (2000). "Beyond computation: information technology, organizational transformations and business performance". Sloan School of Management, MIT. Mimeo.

Cantwell J (1995). "The globalisation of technology: what remains of the product cycle model?", *Cambridge Journal of Economics* 19: 155-174.

Chandler AD (1977). *The Visible Hand: The Managerial Revolution in American Business.* Cambridge, MA: The Belknap Press of Harvard University Press.

Chesbrough HW (2003). *Open Innovation: The New Imperative for Creating and Profiting from Technology.* Boston, MA: Harvard Business School Press.

Christensen CM (1997). *The Innovator's Dilemma: When New Technologies Cause Great Firms to Fail.* Boston, MA: Harvard Business School Press.

D'Costa AP (2004). "Globalization, development, and mobility of technical talent: India and Japan in comparative perspectives". *Research paper* 2004/62, World Institute for Development Economics Research (WIDER), United Nations University (UNU).

Dunning, JH (1998). "Globalization, technology and space". In Chandler AD et al., eds., *The Dynamic Firm: The Role of Technology, Strategy, Organization, and Regions.* Oxford and New York: Oxford University Press.

Ernst D (1997). "From partial to systemic globalization: international production networks in the electronics industry". Report to the Sloan Foundation, published as *The Data Storage Industry Globalization Project Report 97-02*, Graduate School of International Relations and Pacific Studies, University of California at San Diego.

_____ (2000). "Inter-organizational knowledge outsourcing: what permits small Taiwanese firms to compete in the computer industry?", *Asia Pacific Journal of Management* 17(2): 223 - 255.

_____ (2002a). "Global production networks and the changing geography of innovation systems. implications for developing countries", *Economics of Innovation and New Technologies* XI(6): 497-523.

_____ (2002b). "The economics of electronics industry: competitive dynamics and industrial organization, in Lazonick W, ed., *The International Encyclopedia of Business and Management* (IEBM), *Handbook of Economics*. London: International Thomson Business Press.

_____ (2003a). "Digital information systems and global flagship networks: how mobile is knowledge in the global network economy?" In Christensen JF, ed., *The Industrial Dynamics of the New Digital Economy*. Cheltenham: Edward Elgar.

_____ (2003b). "Global production networks and industrial upgrading – Malaysia's electronics industry", In Kidd J and Richter FJ, eds., *Trust and Anti-Trust in Cross-Cultural Alliances*. London: Palgrave.

_____ (2004). "Global Production networks in East Asia's electronics industry and upgrading perspectives in Malaysia". In Yusuf S, Altaf MA and Nabeshima K, eds., *Global Production Networking and Technological Change in East Asia*. Washington, D.C.: World Bank and Oxford and New York: Oxford University Press.

_____ (2005a). "Has high-tech, high value-added outsourcing worked?" Invited paper at the Council on Foreign Relations conference on "The Evolving Global Talent Pool: Issues, Challenges and Strategic Implications", New York, 16-17 June.

_____ (2005b). "The new mobility of knowledge: digital information systems and global flagship networks". In Sassen S, ed., *Digital Formations in a Connected World*. Published for the U.S. Social Science Research Council, Princeton, NJ: Princeton University Press.

_____ (2005c). "Searching for a new role in East Asian regionalization – Japanese production networks in the electronics industry". In Katzenstein P and J and Shiraishi T, eds., *Remaking East Asia: Beyond Americanization and Japanization*. Ithaca, NY: Cornell University Press.

_____ and Kim L (2002). "Global production networks, knowledge diffusion, and local capability formation," *Research Policy* 31(8-9): 1417-1429.

Flaherty T (1986). "Coordinating international manufacturing and technology". In Porter M, ed., *Competition in Global Industries*. Boston, MA: Harvard Business School Press.

Friedman TL (2005). "It's a flat world, after all", *The New York Times* 3 April: 32-38.

Granstrand O and Sjölander S (1990). "Managing innovation in multi-technology corporations", *Research Policy* 19(1): 35-60.

Grindley PC and Teece DJ (1997). "Licensing and cross-licensing in semiconductors and electronics" *California Management Review* 39(2): 8-41.

Grove AS (1996). *Only the Paranoid Survive: How to Exploit the Crisis Points that Challenge Every Company and Career*. New York and London: Harper Collins.

Hagstrøm P (2000). "New wine in old bottles: information technology evolution in firm strategy and structure". In Birkinshaw J and Hagstrøm P, eds., *The Flexible Firm: Capability Management in Network Organizations*. Oxford: Oxford University Press: 194-206.

Hedlund G (1986). "The hypermodern MNC: a heterarchy?", *Human Resource Management* 25: 9-35.

Hyde A (2003). *Working in Silicon Valley – Economic and Legal Analysis of a High-Velocity Labor Market*. Armonk NY: M.E. Sharpe.

Iansiti M (1997). *Technology Integration: Making Critical Choices in a Dynamic World*. Boston, MA: Harvard Business School Press.

_____ and West J (1997). "Technology integration: turning great research into great products", *Harvard Business Review* (May-June): 69-79.

ITRS (2002). *International Technology Roadmap for Semiconductors 2001 Edition*. Austin, TX: Semiconductor Industry Association.

Kobrin SJ (1997). "The architecture of globalization: state sovereignty in a networked global economy". In Dunning JH, ed., *Governments, Globalization and International Business*. Oxford and New York: Oxford University Press.

Kogut B (1985). "Designing global strategies: profiting from operational flexibility", *Sloan Management Review* 27(1): 27-38.

_____ (1989). "A note on global strategies", *Strategic Management Journal* 10: 383-389.

_____ and Kulatilaka N (1994). "Operating flexibility, global manufacturing, and the option value of a multinational network", *Management Science* 40(1): 123-139.

_____ and Zander U (1993). "Knowledge of the firm and the evolutionary theory of the multinational corporation", *Journal of International Business Studies* 24(4): 625-645.

Kuemmerle W (1996). "Home base and foreign direct investment in R&D". Ph.D. dissertation, Harvard Business School, Cambridge, MA.

Lazonick W (2003). "Stock options as a mode of high-tech compensation". Working paper, INSEAD, Fontainebleau.

_____ (2005). "Evolution of the New Economy business model". In Brousseau E and Curien N, eds., *The Economics of the Internet*. Cambridge: Cambridge University Press.

Le Bas C and Sierra C (2002). "Location versus home country advantages in R&D activities: some further results on multinationals' location strategies", *Research Policy* 31(4): 589-609.

Lipsey RG and Carlaw KI (forthcoming). "GPT-driven, endogenous growth", *Economic Journal* forthcoming.

Moore GE (1965). "Cramming more components onto integrated circuits", *Electronics* 38(8):114-117.

Patel P and Pavitt K (1991). "Large firms in the production of the world's technology: an important case of non-globalization", *Journal of International Business Studies* 22(1): 1-21.

_____ and Vega M (1999). "Patterns of internationalisation of corporate technology: location vs. home country advantages", *Research Policy* 28(2-3): 145-155.

Penrose E ([1959] 1995). *The Theory of the Growth of the Firm.* Oxford and New York: Oxford University Press.

Porter ME (1990). *The Competitive Advantage of Nations.* London: Macmillan.

Santos J, Doz Y and Williamson P (2004). "Is your innovation process global?", *MIT Sloan Management Review* 45(4): 31-37.

Stigler G (1951). "The division of labor is limited by the extent of the market", *Journal of Political Economy* 59: 185-193.

Teece DJ (1986). "Transactions cost economics and the multinational enterprise", *Journal of Economic Behavior & Organization* 7: 21-45.

_____ (2000). *Managing Intellectual Capital.* Oxford: Oxford University Press.

United States, Department of Commerce (2003). *The Digital Economy 2003.* Washington, D.C.: Department of Commerce.

United States, NSF (2004). *Science and Engineering Indicators 2004,* volume I. Arlington, VA: National Science Foundation

Williamson OE (1975). *Markets and Hierarchies: Analysis and Antitrust Implications.* New York: The Free Press.

_____ (1985). *The Economic Institutions of Capitalism. Firms, Markets, Relational Contracting.* New York: The Free Press.

Zander U and Kogut B (1995). "Knowledge and the speed of the transfer and imitation of organizational capabilities: an empirical test", *Organizational Science* 5(1): 76-92.

R&D-related FDI in developing countries: implications for host countries

Prasada Reddy[1]

The internationalization of R&D is not a recent phenomenon. Since the 1960s, companies have been performing some kind of R&D activities outside their home countries for various reasons but, the magnitude, nature and scope of the overseas R&D performed in the past were limited. Much of such R&D was undertaken either to facilitate technology transfer by adapting parent firms' technology to local operating conditions or, to gain a greater share of the local markets by developing products that met the preferences of the local customers better.

In the 1990s, the globalization of corporate R&D attracted greater attention of economists and policy makers, mainly due to its changing features and its potential implications. The scope of work in overseas R&D units of TNCs has gone beyond adaptation tasks to encompass innovatory product development for global markets or even the performance of basic research to develop generic technologies.

The objective of this paper is to analyze the driving forces behind R&D-related FDI in developing countries by TNCs and its implications for the developing host countries, particularly for building up innovation capability.

1. Patterns and motives of the globalization of R&D

There are wide differences in the degree of globalization of corporate R&D between different industries. In

---

[1] The views expressed in this study are those of the author and do not necessarily reflect the views of the United Nations, its Member States, or the Institutions to which the author is affiliated.

general, it is observed that technology-intensive industries, such as electronics, biotechnology, chemicals and pharmaceuticals tend to internationalize their strategic R&D to a greater degree than other industries (Reddy 1997). Globally, the pharmaceutical industry, followed by food and beverages, machinery, and transportation equipment manufacturing, show the highest levels of internationalization of R&D (Niosi 1999). In the case of Japanese TNCs, most of their R&D units abroad are in the electronic equipment, pharmaceutical and automotive industries (Odagiri and Yasuda 1996).

The significant increase in the overseas R&D activities of TNCs in recent years was motivated mainly by TNCs' aims to attain global competitiveness. Their new strategic approach involves recasting the roles of individual affiliates and their intra-group interdependencies. In the traditional approach, the scope of R&D performed by an affiliate had to fit within the framework of the bilateral relationship between the parent and the individual affiliate. However, the new approach involves performance of distinctive operations in a framework of interdependent networks of mutually supportive facilities (Pearce 1999: 160).

The growing trend of international technological alliances is another important element in the globalization of R&D. The traditional approach, using transaction costs as the basis, viewed that TNCs tend to develop technology in-house and internalize within their corporate networks by transferring technology to their own affiliates, rather than selling it to other companies. However, since the late 1980s, TNCs have been entering into technological alliances with foreign companies and research institutes in an effort to develop new technologies and products. This new strategy runs contrary to the strategy of internalization. Such alliances are viewed as evolving strategies of the TNCs, designed to successfully compete in a turbulent business environment.

According to Pearce (1999: 157) the growing importance of overseas R&D units in TNCs' strategies reflects:
- an increasing involvement in product development, at the expense of adaptation;
- an interdependent, rather than dependent, position of overseas laboratories in TNCs' technology programmes;
- increased relevance of supply-side influences (host country technology competencies, capacities and heritage); and,
- a decline of centralizing forces on R&D (e.g. economies of scale, communication and co-ordination problems, concerns of knowledge security).

The selection of locations for R&D by TNCs depends on several criteria. These include: proximity to a manufacturing site; the availability of local universities and professionals; the ability to build up a critical mass of local researchers (critical for global technological research); the attractiveness of sources of technical excellence, e.g. universities, customers or suppliers etc. and, the availability of excellent communication systems (de Meyer and Mizushima 1989). The choice of location of R&D also depends on the type of technology to be developed and the advantages of national scientific capacity. For instance, the United Kingdom has been attracting significant foreign R&D investments in the pharmaceutical industry, because of its high quality skills in the life sciences and in chemistry. Similarly, Germany has been a centre for foreign R&D activities in the electrical engineering and electronics industries, reflecting German excellence in these areas (Wortmann 1990).

The scope and level of technological activities carried out abroad by TNCs are determined by the national capabilities of both home and host countries. Cantwell and Janne (1999) suggest that when TNCs based in countries with more advanced technological capabilities in a given industry invest in less advanced countries in the same industry, they tend to differentiate their technological activities. Conversely, when TNCs based in less advanced countries move R&D abroad, they tend to specialize within the same areas as the parent company at home. They also suggest that the TNCs located in leading centres of excellence of a particular industry tend to build up specialization on the basis of the local technological capabilities in host countries. At the same time, TNCs located in less advanced centres tend to draw more on their home-country capabilities, by replicating their home specialization abroad.

The globalization of corporate R&D has been mainly limited to location of R&D units between developed countries but, globalization of corporate R&D continues to evolve as a phenomenon. In recent years, the globalization processes have been encompassing more industries, as well as more geographical areas. Hitherto uncommon locations are attracting R&D-related FDI by TNCs (Reddy 1993).

Since the mid-1980s, as an offshoot of the globalization of corporate R&D, TNCs have started performing some of their strategic R&D in some developing countries. TNCs involved in this new trend seem to be mostly those dealing with new technologies. This strategic move by TNCs is facilitated by the availability of large pools of trained manpower, at substantially lower wages compared to their counterparts in developed countries and, an adequate infrastructure.

The primary driving forces behind the new trends are:
- technology-related motives, i.e. to gain access to foreign science and technology (S&T) resources;
- cost-related motives, i.e. to exploit the cost differentials between different countries and,
- organization-related motives, i.e. rationalization of TNCs' internal operations, where an affiliate in a developing country is assigned a regional or a global product mandate.

The performance of strategic R&D, aimed at developing products for global/regional markets or mission-oriented basic research by TNCs, has implications for the innovatory capabilities of developing host countries (Reddy 1993).

2. Types of R&D units

The different types of R&D activities carried out by foreign affiliates of TNCs can be categorized into:

- Technology-transfer units, which facilitate the transfer of parents' technology to affiliates and, provide local technical services.
- Indigenous technology units, which develop new products for the local market, drawing on local technology.
- Global technology units, which develop new products and processes for main world markets.
- Corporate technology units, which generate basic technology of a long-term or exploratory nature for use by the parent company (Ronstadt 1977).
- Regional technology units, which develop products for regional markets. While markets worldwide are integrating in terms of standards and technologies, some regional clusters are also emerging. National markets in these regional clusters share some common features and needs for specialized products. Examples of this can be found in biotechnology, food processing (special types of food, taste, etc.), pharmaceuticals (drugs for regional diseases) or, in software development (Reddy and Sigurdson 1994).

3. Waves of R&D globalization

The evolution of the globalization of R&D can be analyzed in terms of waves (phases). Such a framework helps in a comprehensive understanding of globalization as a broader process, by analysing the driving forces in each time period, the type of R&D located abroad and, the potential impact on the host countries. Each wave represents a set of distinctive characteristic features, yet reveals the continuation from one wave to the other (Reddy 2000: 52-56). The division of time periods should be taken as approximate indications and not as precise cut-off dates.

a. The beginnings of the internationalization of R&D – the first wave in the 1960s

The number of firms performing R&D abroad in the 1960s and earlier was extremely small. Most of the R&D performed abroad was that of technology-transfer units. The driving force during this *first wave* was to gain entry into a market abroad. This required the adaptation of the product and process technologies to local conditions and the need for the continuous support of technical services. The establishment of technology-transfer units was considered a more cost-effective way of dealing with technical problems than sending R&D missions from headquarters. The categories of industries involved in this process were mostly mechanical, electrical and engineering, including automobile industries.

b. The growth of international corporate R&D –the second wave in the 1970s

By the 1970s, firms had started performing R&D abroad in a significant way. The main driving force was to increase the local market share abroad. This required increased sensitivity to local market differences to enhance competitiveness and TNCs' general move towards serving world markets. This was reflected in the fact that most of the R&D units abroad had been established through acquisitions of companies abroad (Behrman and Fischer 1980). Moreover, host-country governments, using industrial policies stipulating local-content, re-export or plant-location requirements, started pressurizing TNCs to increase technology transfer. These circumstances triggered what can be considered the *second wave* of the internationalization of R&D, which differed from the earlier wave in that an increasing number of indigenous technology units were set up to develop new and improved products for   local markets. This type of activity was predominant in branded and packaged consumer goods, chemicals and allied products, etc.

c. From internationalization to globalization of R&D –the third wave in the 1980s

A number of major changes have been taking place since the 1980s in the nature and scope of R&D undertaken abroad by TNCs. Increasingly higher-order R&D, such as regional technology units, global technology units and corporate technology units, had been located abroad in what can be regarded as the *third wave* of globalization of R&D. Such R&D abroad is carried out as part of long-term corporate strategy and is often carried out through inter-organizational collaboration. Hence, the change in the term from internationalization to globalization, reflecting the characteristic differences from the earlier waves. The main driving forces for this phenomenon had been:

- first, the increasingly globalized basis of competition, aided by the convergence of consumer preferences worldwide, creating a need for learning;
- second, the increasing science-base of new technologies, necessitating multi-sourcing of technologies;
- third, the rationalization of TNCs' operations, assigning specific global roles to their affiliates abroad.

These trends are visible mainly in microelectronics, pharmaceuticals, biotechnology and new materials. The improvement of information and communication technologies and the flexibility of new science-based technologies, that allow de-linking of R&D and manufacturing activities, vastly facilitated this globalization process.

d. The evolving patterns of globalization of R&D -the fourth wave in the 1990s

The key driving forces for globalization of R&D since the 1990s have been the increasing demand for skilled scientists and rising R&D costs. These forces are triggering the *fourth wave* of globalization of R&D, encompassing some developing economies and countries in transition. The mismatch between the outputs of universities and the needs of industry is giving rise to shortages of research personnel throughout the developed world, especially in engineering fields related to electronics, automation and computer-aided development/manufacturing (OECD 1988), compelling companies to widen their research networks in order to tap more geographically dispersed scientific talent. The existence of an international market for investments in research, education and scientific and engineering personnel and the necessity of scientific knowledge for competitiveness are leading corporations to direct their investments to those geographical areas which can best meet their research needs, including developing countries. TNCs are also sensitive to variations in the cost of R&D inputs from country to country (Mansfield et al. 1979). This move by TNCs is facilitated by the availability of large pools of scientifically and technically trained manpower in these countries at substantially lower wages *vis-à-vis* the developed countries. The categories of industries involved are microelectronics, biotechnology, pharmaceuticals, chemicals and software.

4. Implications for developing host countries

A few studies have been done on the impact of TNCs' R&D activities on the host country. Whatever the implications suggested by these studies, they tend to be postulated as hypotheses. Whether the performance of R&D by TNCs contributes to the enhancement or retardation of independent technological capability of the host country is a complicated issue.

In general, there are now two opposing views regarding the impact of TNCs' R&D on the host countries. One view considers inward R&D-related FDI to be beneficial to economic growth, by providing technology and managerial skills, which in turn create indirect positive effects for the host country at a lower cost. These positive effects include technical support to local suppliers and customers and contract jobs from foreign R&D units to local R&D organizations, etc. The counter view argues that R&D activities by foreign firms tend to tap into unique local R&D resources with little or no benefit to the host country. Concentrating on problems of little relevance to the local economy, they may be a little more than disguised "brain-drain", diverting scarce technical resources from more useful purposes (Dunning 1992).

In the context of developing countries, where the scientific and technical resources are underutilized, the counterview may lose strength. The benefits are larger, while the costs involved may be smaller. In the case of developing host countries, the cost factor may be that such R&D activities may create islands of high-technology enclaves with little diffusion of knowledge into the economy. However, over the long term knowledge and skills cannot be isolated. The mobility of researchers, the need for local procurement of persons and materials etc. are bound to diffuse technologies throughout the economy (Reddy 1993).

In general an R&D affiliate is expected to benefit the host country in three ways (Pearce 1989).

- By adapting products and processes to local conditions, it improves the efficiency of the local manufacturing facilities. This, in turn, may benefit the host country by increasing the size of output, employment and tax revenue and, the consumers would have access to products better suited to their requirements, at perhaps a lower price.

- By assisting the local production affiliate to introduce a new product, R&D may help to improve the export performance of the affiliate.

- Through its linkages with the local S&T community, an R&D unit derives benefit as well as contributing to the widening of the scope of capabilities of local S&T resources.

While analysing the implications for the host countries, it is important to consider the type of R&D being performed and its direct and indirect effects. Depending on the type of R&D being carried out, the impact on the host country varies. Each type of R&D unit displays distinctive linkages with the local affiliate, the corporate headquarters and, with the local science and technology system. The stronger the ties with the local organizations, be it the firms or research institutes, the greater will be the diffusion of technology/knowledge into the host country.

The ties are virtually non-existent for a technology-transfer unit, whose main technology links are with the parent; somewhat strong for an indigenous technology unit, which may (but not always) to some extent draw on the local science and technology system to develop products particularly designed for the local market. In this type of R&D unit, its linkages with the local marketing function assume greater importance than linkages with the local S&T system; stronger for a global technology unit and strongest for a corporate technology unit. In these two types of R&D units, the primary motive being that of exploiting local sources of S&T that cannot be accessed easily from outside the country, strong local linkages are established (Westney 1988).

The quantity and quality of R&D performed abroad by a TNC, i.e. the degree of globalization depends on the type and cost of knowledge available abroad that is complementary to the TNC's operations, i.e. the degree of complementarity. The larger the degree of complementarity available abroad, the larger the degree of globalization. Similarly, the degree of integration of TNCs' activities in a host country depends on the degree of complementarity provided by that country. The larger the degree of complementary knowledge or skills available in a host country, the larger is the degree of integration. TNCs tend to locate R&D in countries that offer a knowledge base that is complementary to their home country's knowledge base. This is mainly because the home country still remains the base for the largest proportion of R&D activities and, a TNC by globalizing R&D either seeks to overcome shortages of specific inputs in the home country or, expand its knowledge base into related activities. So the larger the degree of complementarity between the home country and host country, the larger is the degree of globalization from the home country and the larger is the degree of integration with the host country.

On one hand, the location of R&D facilities by TNCs would increase the size of the technology-base of the host country, through the employment of local research personnel but, on the other hand, the recruitment of these resources by TNCs, may pre-empt their availability to domestic firms. The final impact depends on the type of R&D performed by the TNCs, the type of local resources used by them and, the supply conditions for such resources in the host economy (UNCTAD 1995).

The potential impact of R&D-related FDI on a developing host country can be classified into direct effects, spin-off effects and spillover effects.

a. Direct effects

- *Transfer of technology.* R&D-related FDI brings into the host country new equipment (e.g. laboratory machinery and testing equipment), transfer of application knowledge and new research methodologies to local scientists and engineers, and know-how relating to R&D management etc. While scientists and engineers in developing countries do possess the basic scientific and engineering knowledge, they often lack the skills to convert this knowledge into tangible products and processes. An inflow of R&D-related FDI helps the host country personnel in acquiring such application knowledge.

- *Subcontracting R&D to local research institutes and firms.* Depending on the type of R&D being conducted by an affiliate, it may sponsor research projects in local universities, by providing finances, equipment and training. For instance, the pharmaceutical TNC GlaxoSmithKline established a trust fund (S$31 million) for a drug-screening centre and another (S$30 million) for a neurobiology laboratory focusing on the brain in the Institute of Molecular and Cell Biology in Singapore.

b. Spin-off effects

- *Transfer of technology to local firms.* R&D affiliates of TNCs may transfer some technologies developed by them to local firms. During the course of R&D, an affiliate may develop some by-products that the TNC may not want to keep for itself. In such cases an affiliate may transfer such technologies to local firms for commercialization. For instance, AstraZeneca's Research Centre India spent its initial two years of its establishment in developing reagents (the basic tools of recombinant DNA research) and transferred these technologies to two local scientists in India, who established a new company called GENEI (Gene

India) to commercialize these products. Prior to the establishment of GENEI, these products were being imported in refrigerated containers, which added costs and delays to biotechnology research in India. Now GENEI exports these products to several countries, including the United States. From being a net importer of these products, India has now become a net exporter. In addition, other organizations in India involved in biotechnology research benefit from low costs supplies and also avoid delays associated with imports. AstraZeneca gains by securing regular supplies at low costs.

- *Emergence of spin-off firms set up by former employees.* There are several cases of scientists working in an R&D affiliate leaving the TNC to set up their own subcontract R&D firms. The technical, commercial and managerial knowledge gained through work in the affiliate helps these scientists in setting up such new firms. Affiliates often support such former employees through awarding R&D contracts to them. For instance, Parallax Research of Singapore was established by a former research engineer of Hewlett Packard. Parallax now carries out subcontracted R&D for several TNCs, including Hewlett Packard, in the areas of mechanical and electromechanical systems design and development. For example, under such a subcontract Parallax designed and developed an integrated chip for infrared communications exclusively for Hewlett Packard.

- *Acquisition of new skills and knowledge by supplier firms.* TNCs' R&D activities are placing demands on their suppliers in host countries for new products and services. Consequently, these suppliers in the host countries are acquiring new skills and knowledge necessary to meet such demand either from other organizations located within the country and abroad or developing such products and services on their own. For instance, the inflow of R&D-related FDI placed demands on Indian architect firms to acquire new skills. The construction of R&D laboratories requires high technologies and skills (e.g. laboratories need to have rooms with highly sterile environments and/or rooms that can withstand earthquakes and fire and, are also aesthetically inspiring to researchers). Faced with this challenge, Indian architect firms have acquired these new skills/knowledge and are now competing for such contracts abroad.

c. Spillover effects

- *The emergence of a new class of entrepreneur.* One of the most important benefits is that international corporate R&D activities are infusing the scientific community in developing countries with commercial culture. R&D-related FDI opened up new opportunities for scientists and engineers in developing countries by training them in converting their theoretical knowledge into tangible products and processes and, by providing them with opportunities to become entrepreneurs by helping them set up subcontract R&D firms. The examples of GENEI and Parallax reflect this trend.

- *The emergence of an R&D culture in developing host countries.* Inflows of R&D-related FDI reinforce the R&D culture of the host economies. Local firms in host countries also tend to take up or increase innovation activities due to the demonstration effect of TNCs' R&D affiliates. For instance, although precise figures are not available, the R&D spending by Indian companies has gone up significantly since the 1990s, when the R&D-related FDI by TNCs started flowing into India. This is reflected in the increasing number of national and international patents granted to Indian companies and research institutes. India's spending on R&D as a proportion of GDP has also gone up to more than one per cent mainly because of private sector spending on R&D.

- *Competition for R&D personnel.* R&D affiliates of TNCs tend to attract the cream of the scientists and engineers in developing host countries through higher pay, better career prospects and challenging tasks. This leaves only the relatively less talented people for recruitment by host countries' firms and research institutes. This may affect the quality and quantity of R&D focused on national social and economic objectives. However, this negative effect is mitigated to a large extent through the mobility of people from TNCs' affiliates to set up their own firms or join other large local firms at a more senior level.

5. Conclusion

The emergence of R&D-related FDI seems to offer some fresh opportunities for developing host countries. R&D investments can bring international prestige as well as employment opportunities for the highly educated. Potentially, international R&D would be also an impetus to the R&D being performed by the indigenous industry. Moreover, by creating a proper framework, developing host countries could persuade the TNCs to commercialize the research results in the country, making the benefits larger and quicker. However, for the host economy to show substantial improvements, the capabilities of the majority of the population must be enhanced.

References

Behrman JN and Fischer W A (1980). *Overseas R&D Activities of Transnational Companies.* Cambridge, MA: Oelgeschlager, Gunn & Hain.

Cantwell, J and Janne O (1999). "Technological globalisation and innovative centres: the role of corporate technological leadership and locational hierarchy", *Research Policy* 28(2-3): 119-144.

de Meyer A and Mizushima A. (1989). "Global R&D management", *R&D Management* 19(2): 135-146.

Dunning JH (1992). "Multinational enterprises and the globalisation of innovatory capacity". In Granstrand O, Håkanson L and Sjölander S, eds., *Technology Management and International Business: Internationalisation of R&D and Technology.* Chichester: John Wiley & Sons: 19-51.

Mansfield E, Teece D and Romeo A (1979). "Overseas research and development by US-based firms", *Economica* 46: 187-196.

Niosi J (1999). "Introduction – The internationalization of industrial R&D: from technology transfer to the learning organization", *Research Policy* 28(2-3): 107-117.

Odagiri H and Yasuda H (1996). "The determinants of overseas R&D by Japanese firms: an empirical study at the industry and company levels", *Research Policy* 25: 1059-1079.

OECD (1988). *Science and Technology Policy Outlook 1988.* Paris: Organisation for Economic Cooperation and Development.

Pearce RD (1999). "Decentralized R&D and strategic competitiveness: globalised approaches to generation and use of technology in multinational enterprises (MNEs)", *Research Policy* 28(2-3): 151-178.

_____ (1989). *The Internationalisation of Research and Development by Multinational Enterprises.* London: Macmillan.

Reddy ASP and Sigurdson J (1994). "Emerging patterns of globalisation of corporate R&D and scope for innovation capability building in developing countries?", *Science and Public Policy* 21(5): 283-294.

Reddy P (2000). *Globalization of Corporate R&D: Implications for innovation systems in host countries.* London and New York: Routledge.

_____ (1997). "New trends in globalization of corporate R&D and implications for innovation capability in host countries: a survey from India", *World Development* 25(11): 1821-1837.

_____ (1993). "Emerging patterns of internationalisation of corporate R&D: opportunities for developing countries?" In Brundenius C and Göransson B, eds., *New Technologies and Global Restructuring: The Third World at a Crossroads.* London: Taylor Graham.

Ronstadt R (1977). *Research and Development Abroad by US Multinationals.* New York: Praeger.

UNCTAD (1995). *World Investment Report 1995: Transnational corporations and competitiveness.* New York and Geneva: United Nations, United Nations publication, Sales No. E.95.II.A.7.

Westney DE (1988). "International and external linkages in the MNC: the case of R&D subsidiaries in Japan". *Working Paper* 1973-88, Massachusetts, Sloan School of Management, MIT.

Wortmann M (1990). "Multinationals and the internationalisation of R&D: new developments in German companies", *Research Policy* 19: 175-183.

PART II

Case studies

Features and impacts of the internationalization of R&D by transnational corporations: China's case

Zhou Yuan[1]

In recent years, an increasing number of TNCs have established R&D laboratories and increased their R&D spending in China. This paper suggests that this internationalization of R&D by TNCs can benefit developing countries such as China, although it cannot automatically upgrade the local S&T capabilities. Therefore, China must upgrade, in parallel to FDI in R&D, its S&T competitiveness by strengthening its national innovatory capacities.

1. R&D laboratories of TNCs in China

Since Nortel Networks Corporation and Beijing University of Posts and Telecommunications jointly set up an R&D centre in 1994, the number of TNCs' R&D laboratories in China has been growing steadily. This tendency was especially pronounced in recent years. Statistics collected by the Ministry of Science and Technology show that in 2002, more than 100 R&D laboratories were established by TNCs in China, and by the end of June, 2004, over 600 of the world's best-known TNCs had set up their R&D laboratories in China.

In 2002, the Beijing Municipal Science and Technology Commission carried out a sample survey among 82 R&D laboratories of TNCs. That survey (China, MOST 2002) concluded that:

- many large and well-known TNCs had set up R&D laboratories in China. Of the 82 sample laboratories, 55 had been set up by *Fortune Global 500* TNCs;

---

[1] The views expressed in this study are those of the author and do not necessarily reflect the views of the United Nations, its Member States, or the Institutions to which the author is affiliated.

- TNCs' R&D laboratories in China were unevenly distributed: metropolises with relatively strong R&D capacities, such as Beijing, Shanghai, Guangzhou, Shenzhen, Xian and Chengdu, were by far the most attractive locations for R&D. According to the survey, 60% of the R&D laboratories of foreign TNCs were located in Beijing, 18% in Shanghai and 6% in Shenzhen;
- TNCs' R&D laboratories were active mostly in high-technology industries, such as information technologies, software and computers (58 laboratories), the chemical industry (9), pharmaceuticals (7) and the automotive industry (5);
- the majority of the parent companies of the 82 R&D laboratories were headquartered in the United States (32), Europe (20) and Japan (18); these three locations together accounted for 85% of the headquarters. The Republic of Korea, Hong Kong (China) and Taiwan Province of China were found to be additional important sources of R&D by TNCs.

TNCs invest increasing amounts of financial resources into R&D in China. In 1999, of the 10 TNCs in Pudong, Shanghai, whose output was in the range of RMB 1 to 6 billion, only four spent more than RMB 100 million on R&D. By 2004, Motorola alone had invested about RMB 1.3 billion in R&D. R&D activities supported by foreign investment are playing an increasingly important role in China. In 2000, the proportion of foreign investment to overall R&D expenditure surpassed that of Germany and Japan; the ratio in China is relatively high in manufacturing (OECD 2003 and China, MOST 2002).

2. Reasons to invest in R&D in China

The boom of R&D is driven largely by the abundant S&T human resources of China. Some TNCs like IBM and Microsoft Research evaluate their R&D laboratories as a fundamental part of their global R&D activities. The mission of these R&D laboratories is to become an international R&D centre, rather than a support laboratory serving the local market. These R&D laboratories value not only the Chinese market, but also available talents and technological capacities.

The advantages of Beijing and Shanghai in particular, lie in the great number of colleges and universities located there, their large pool of S&T talents and, their well-developed industries.

A second reason to invest in R&D in China is to capture its huge internal market. Serving as a link between the advanced technology of the TNCs and the specific demands of China, R&D laboratories can adapt foreign products and technologies to local needs. For instance, a local R&D laboratory of Matsushita Electric Works adapts the technology of the parent corporation for electrical appliances to Chinese specifications. With that adaptation, Matsushita has gained a good share of the Chinese market.

3. Forms of R&D laboratories in China

The following are the three most common forms of TNCs' R&D laboratories in China.

• The first form is an independent R&D laboratory. This is the most mature, popular and advanced type, and is also the core of TNCs' R&D activities in China. Those laboratories are branches of global R&D networks of TNCs, under the direct management of the R&D headquarters, and are financed by the TNCs. As this kind of R&D laboratory can better protect intellectual property rights, TNCs, attracted by the improving investment environment, tend to establish this type of R&D laboratory in China. By the end of

October 2003, more than 260 independent R&D laboratories had been established by TNCs in China.[2]

- The second is an R&D department, either under a business section or, under a joint venture, or undertaking R&D activities without establishing a specialized department. Many TNCs try to improve their products and services in order to better gear their products to local demand. Motorola, for instance, established R&D departments in the Personal Communications Sector and the Global Telecom Solutions Sector respectively, to carry out specific R&D studies. Moreover, since most foreign affiliates in China are high-technology companies, almost all of these enterprises have their own R&D departments or technology development support companies, in order to ensure normal production and introduce internationally advanced technologies. Foreign affiliates producing software in particular, need a number of personnel to carry out R&D activities; accordingly, they invest in R&D activities, although they do not necessarily have an independent R&D department. This is popular among small foreign affiliates in software development.

- The third form is a cooperative R&D unit with Chinese universities, R&D laboratories and enterprises. A limited number of TNCs subcontract some R&D to local higher learning R&D laboratories and enterprises, taking advantage of their personnel. A survey among foreign enterprises undertaken by the Chinese Academy of Social Sciences shows that 77% of the foreign enterprises had never formally cooperated with Chinese R&D laboratories and 79% of them did not have any plan in this regard.

---

[2] According to the statistics of the Ministry of Science and Technology.

4. Impacts of R&D laboratories of TNCs on China

TNCs' investment in R&D in China has had a positive impact on the development of human resources, R&D management and on industrial technology. On the other hand, it may have had a negative impact on Chinese R&D laboratories.

a. Positive impacts

First of all, TNCs' investment in R&D has resulted in the development of human resources on a large scale. TNCs emphasize the training of personnel, and regard improving the quality of personnel as a key factor of their competitiveness. Although China has abundant R&D personnel, most of these talents used to end up in higher learning and R&D laboratories to undertake basic research. Moreover, these talents did not meet the demands of the market. TNCs offer them relevant training. This contributes to the development of Chinese human resources and the enhancement of their talents.

Second, R&D laboratories established by TNCs bring advanced R&D management to China. TNCs not only have experience with advanced innovation systems and global innovation networks, but also with developed management systems and methods of R&D networking. Therefore, TNCs' R&D, and the training of local people who have been involved in TNCs' R&D management, can have a positive spillover effect on the R&D management of Chinese institutes and enterprises. In a short period of time, for instance, Microsoft Research Asia developed an excellent software R&D laboratory with a worldwide reputation and, it might be possible to emulate some of the methods used to achieve this.

Third, TNCs' R&D laboratories raise the overall level of industrial technology in China and contribute to the adjustment of its industrial structure. As TNCs' R&D

laboratories are technology intensive, TNCs increase the overall industrial technology level of the economy by carrying on R&D activities and applying for patents in the area of their activities. Their output of S&T development and innovation may give birth to the development of relevant products along the product chain, and also produce spillover effects on product and technique innovation.

b. Negative impacts

TNCs' R&D laboratories can also exert a negative impact on Chinese R&D.

- Chinese R&D laboratories may find it more difficult to hire talent attracted by TNC laboratories.
- There is a risk that State technological secrets might be disclosed to foreign firms as a result of personnel movements and in-depth cooperation with TNCs.
- Some less efficient local R&D laboratories may be forced to close down because of strong competition by TNCs. In cases of calls for public bids for instance, foreign affiliates may be in a better position to win due to their advanced research capability, equipment and management experience. The trend of crowding out local laboratories might increase after China's accession to the World Trade Organization.
- The internationalization of TNCs' R&D alone cannot upgrade China's S&T competitiveness. The level of diffusion of the competitive technology of TNCs in China is still low. According to a survey undertaken by the Chinese Academy of Social Sciences in Beijing, Shanghai, Suzhou and Donguan, 91% of foreign affiliates do not apply for patents, and 13% apply for international patents only. Moreover, most of the TNCs' R&D expenditure is within their own affiliates. In 2002, Chinese universities and public laboratories derived a mere 1% of their resources

from foreign TNCs and their affiliates.[3] From the point of view of the structure of R&D expenditure by foreign TNCs and their affiliates in China, 88% was devoted to business R&D spending, 8% to laboratories and 4% to higher learning (China, MOST 2002). Thus, TNCs' R&D activities in China focus on applications, rather than basic research undertaken by higher learning and governmental R&D laboratories (the relevant technologies that are decisive to national competitiveness on the macro level).

5. Conclusion

In general, China can benefit from the internationalization of R&D by gaining advanced R&D experience and developing its human resources. Nevertheless, a developing country such as China needs to rely primarily on its own forces to upgrade S&T competitiveness. TNCs' R&D activities alone cannot provide the support needed for national and business S&T competitiveness. The enhancement of China's competitiveness lies first and foremost with the Government of China and Chinese enterprises.

References

China, MOST (2002). *China Science and Technology Indicators 2002*. Beijing: Ministry of Science and Technology (in Chinese).

OECD (2002). *OECD Science, Technology and Industry Outlook 2002*. Paris: Organisation for Economic Co-operation and Development.

---

[3] 76% was derived from government sources, 11% from local firms and 12% from other sources. See China, MOST 2002.

International R&D strategies of TNCs from developing countries: the case of China

Maximilian von Zedtwitz[1]

International R&D is a by-product of intensified merger and acquisition activity (Gerpott 1995) and more deliberate internationalization of corporate innovation (Bartlett and Ghoshal 1989). Research on the latter has provided information on different typologies of corporate technology activities (Medcof 1997), R&D internationalization strategies (see the special issue in *Research Policy* in 1999),[2] R&D location decision-making (Voelker and Stead 1999), multi-site R&D project management and technology transfer (Chiesa 2000), and intra-organizational technical communication (Katz and Allen 1984). Most of this research — with few exceptions — focused on R&D conducted in developed countries, partly because these countries were responsible for the bulk of global R&D conducted, partly because their protagonists were more easily accessible and forthcoming and, partly because R&D in developing countries was insignificant in scale. For instance, a review by von Zedtwitz and Gassmann (2002) indicates that on average, European firms conduct around 30% of their R&D abroad (half of which in other European countries). The same ratio is about 8-12% for United States firms and no more than 5% for Japanese firms. Data and research on R&D in developing countries is scattered and few. Only a handful of economies outside the developed countries receive some research attention, among them are Singapore, the Republic of Korea, India and, most recently, China.

The principal research purpose of this paper is to shed more light on R&D internationalization by firms in developing

---

[1] The views expressed in this study are those of the author and do not necessarily reflect the views of the United Nations, its Member States, or the Institutions to which the author is affiliated.

[2] Volume 28, Issues 2-3.

countries, with a focus on China. First, it assesses the extent of international R&D emerging from developing countries, proposing a 2x2 model of past research on international R&D. Based on research conducted on Chinese technology-intensive companies, strategies and struggles of R&D internationalization are investigated and analyzed. The data seems to suggest that due to their special position, firms from a developing country organize their international R&D activities as both capability-enhancing and capability-exploiting structures. The paper concludes with open research areas and some preliminary implications for research, management and policy making.

1. Research framework and directions

R&D has always been considered a domain of firms in technologically advanced and economically developed countries. In fact, the ten largest countries in terms of GDP also lead in terms of technology-intensity (except for China and Brazil). TNCs account for substantial shares (between 33% to 57%, according to a mid-1990s study reported in Gassmann and von Zedtwitz 1999) of their total national R&D expenditures. TNCs dominate private international R&D investments. Of the 100 largest TNCs in the world (in the year 2000), 94 were headquartered in developed countries, three in China, and one each in Mexico, Venezuela, and the Republic of Korea. Patent applications in the most important markets are led in numbers by large TNCs from the United States, Japan, and Western Europe. Clearly, firms in developed countries dominate domestic and international R&D. (Dunning 1988, UNCTAD 1999 and 2001).

R&D in developing countries has figured less prominently. Most research has concentrated on technology transfer to these countries, and their capacity to absorb advanced technologies from abroad (Kim 1980 and 1997, Lall 1990). Without doubt, the level of science, technology, and innovation has been increasing over the last years but, the investment ratios of S&T to GDP are still far behind developed countries (see Schaaper 2004, OECD 2002). Moreover, the leading TNCs from developing countries tend to be low on technology-intensity, and concentrate on natural resources such as real estate, oil & exploration, and mining & materials. R&D by the few technology firms in these countries tends to be comparatively weak. Lack of S&T resources and lack of local market demand for sophisticated and expensive technology goods discourage private efforts in serious R&D.

For the first time since the mid-1980s, when international R&D became a more widespread practice among technology TNCs, we are witnessing the emergence of a new class of high-technology companies from developing countries, most notably India and China. These companies compete in highly technology-intensive industries, in which customers demand great rates of innovation and, in which timely application of technical know-how is paramount. They have one thing in common: they are headquartered in large developing economies. They differ from their predecessors in the Republic of Korea and Japan in that they are facing international competition in their home markets, that technological change has accelerated since the 1970s and, that know-how — and the workforce — has become more mobile. In other words, the environment has become more global.

Competition among these companies can be extremely intense, which does not favour internationalization into foreign markets. However, a few companies have emerged that pursue R&D of international calibre nevertheless, such as Embraer in Brazil (the world's third largest supplier of mid-range aircraft), Huawei (a leading telecommunications firm from China), and Infosys (a global IT services provider in India). The evolution of companies from developing countries, and the development of their innovative capacity has been the subject of recent investigations (Lee et al. 1988, Bell and Pavitt 1993, Sung and Hong 1999, Xie and Wu 2003, Xie and White 2004). However, the extent to which firms from developing countries develop international innovation capacities and build global R&D networks has not yet been studied in detail. Here too the best explanation is that until recently there were probably a very limited number of firms from developing countries able to undertake such international R&D.

Figure 1 summarizes some of the previous research trajectories in international R&D research. The first type concerns "traditional" R&D internationalization among developed countries, i.e. mostly within the triad countries of North America, Western Europe, and Japan. This area of R&D internationalization has been widely researched, and yielded a very valuable and rich literature as well as a fundamental albeit initial understanding of transnational innovation management. Most of the international R&D flows are covered by Type 1 research, as indicated by the preferred routes of FDI (the Triad countries accounted for 71% of all FDI inflows and 82% of all FDI outflows in 2001). However, the rise of China (and to some extend India) as a principal recipient and source of FDI in 2002 and 2003 has led to a new, "modern" category of research, denoted Type 2 in figure 1. Examples of Type 2 R&D internationalization are IBM's establishment of R&D in India, Microsoft's Research laboratory in China and, Fujitsu's Development Center in Malaysia. This modern form of R&D internationalization became popular in the late 1990s, driven in part by improved economic conditions in South-East Asia, China and Central and Eastern Europe, in part by strategic considerations of parent companies to set global standards and build global brands and, in part by a growing understanding and financial commitment of TNCs to support local sales with local R&D efforts.

Figure 1. Types of R&D internationalization, based on the dates of establishment of international laboratories, early 1970s to 2004

	Type 2 MODERN (e.g., US → China, EU → India)	Type 1 TRADITIONAL (e.g., US → EU, JP → US)
Advanced **Home** **Country**		
Developing	Type 4 EXPANSIONARY (e.g., China → Brazil, India → China)	Type 3 CATCH-UP (e.g., China → US, India → EU)

	Developing	**Host** **Country**	Advanced

Source: the author.

Type 3 and 4 in figure 1 denote a novel, so far mostly ignored direction of R&D internationalization. Arguably, researchers such as Lall (1987, 1990) and Kim (1980, 1997) have studied the acquisition and development of technological competencies in developing countries but, the notion of firms headquartered in developing countries establishing R&D capabilities outside their home countries is new. The espoused view was that firms in developing countries were too busy absorbing technology transferred from abroad, and hardly capable to push technological boundaries themselves. They would use their new competitive advantages to defend and build domestic market shares and, if they were sufficiently attractive enough, they would be acquired by much larger foreign TNCs. Some countries imposed policies protecting domestic technology companies, either by making foreign acquisitions more difficult or by curbing competition from foreign affiliates. In any case, the internationalization of business and technology has largely been unidirectional from developed to developing countries.

Figure 2. International R&D units and their classification, based on data collected up to 2004

	Type 2: Modern	Type 1: Traditional
Advanced Home Country	**194 (25%)**	**496 (64%)**
	Type 4: Expansionary	Type 3: Catch-Up
Developing	**22 (3%)**	**64 (8%)**

	Developing	**Host Country**	**Advanced**

Source: Based on own research of the locations of 776 international R&D locations (von Zedwitz and Gassmann 2002).

Type 3 describes firms from a developing country conducting R&D in a developed country. Because of their principal motivation of catching up with developed countries, this type of R&D internationalization is labelled catch-up, with examples such as Samsung of the Republic of Korea investing in R&D in Europe, and Acer of Taiwan Province of China in the United States. These firms are naturally attracted to using developed countries as R&D bases, partly in order to acquire local technology and science, and partly in order to support local product development.

Type 4 R&D internationalization is when a firm in one developing economy invests in R&D in another developing country. The reasons for this kind of investment may be in supporting second-generation technology transfer (when the earlier recipient of a technology transfers a technology on to an even less developed country) or, to support other local business activities. An example is Acer's R&D laboratory in China, and Huawei's R&D centre in Bangalore, India.

As can be seen in figure 2, the instances of Type 3 and 4 internationalization are not trivial. Using a database comprising the locations of 1,269 R&D units, 776 locations were identified as international, meaning that the parent company was headquartered in another country. 64 belonged to Type 3 or the catch-up type, while a respectable 22 belonged to Type 4 or the expansionary type (496 R&D units belonged to Type 1 or the traditional type, and 194 to Type 2 or the modern type of R&D internationalization). At least in this database, international R&D from developing countries already constitutes about 11% of all international R&D.

These Types 3 and 4 of R&D internationalization are not well understood and - to some extent - even contradict established views on international R&D. For instance, firms from developed countries invest in R&D in developing countries in order to exploit labour and operating costs advantages. Hence, under what circumstances would a company from a developing firm consider giving up this particular advantage by going into a country with a highly adverse purchasing power parity or, as long as companies from developing countries are still struggling with the incorporation of mature technologies transferred by joint venture partners, how can they assume that they are ready to absorb far more sophisticated technology currently under development in developed countries? Furthermore, these foreign advanced technologies are probably without differentiation potential for firms from developing countries in the more important domestic markets.

With its high GDP growth rate and rapid industrialization of the coastal areas, as well as a growing number of technology-based companies, China provides a very fitting example of a developing country. China also faces many of the same problems other developing countries need to confront, such as a high degree of state control, low purchasing power of its domestic currency, comparatively low rates of tertiary education and, a lag in developing an economic and legal framework conducive for private business. More specifically, the research presented in this paper pursued the following research questions.

- How significant a role do companies from developing countries, in particular China, play in worldwide R&D? How relevant is this topic for future research?
- What motivates companies from China to conduct R&D elsewhere? What are the push and the pull factors?
- What strategies do Chinese firms employ in order to expand R&D internationally?
- What barriers and challenges do Chinese companies face in doing so that may be more specific to them as being from a developing county?

2. Research methodology

The aim of this analysis was to investigate a well researched phenomenon (internationalization of R&D) in a new environment (China). With this objective, an empirical, quantitative research approach would have been appropriate. However, initial exploratory interviews indicated a low intensity of international R&D in Chinese companies as well as a high disinclination to cooperate in academic research on R&D management. In one of the closest comparables to the present research, Jin Chen of Zhejiang University attempted to study international innovation by Chinese companies but received only 28 valid questionnaires out of 279 sent out (Chen 2003). With response rates this low, and the main focus of the research questions to be qualitative in nature, it was concluded that survey-based research would be ineffective in gathering the information necessary for purely quantitative empirical analysis. Instead, it seemed more fruitful to focus on the top Chinese companies and to conduct in-depth research.

Data for this research was thus collected mostly by personal research interviews, and complemented by database research. Research interviews focused on senior R&D managers in selected Chinese companies, most of which are leading firms in their industry (Lenovo, Huawei, Haier, Kelon, Founder, ZTE, Longshine, China National Petroleum, Datang, Dongfeng, NetEase). Only the first six of these companies operate international R&D units, while the last five did not posses foreign R&D presence at the end of 2004. However, both groups were investigated, as the research objective also included the identification of barriers and challenges of R&D internationalization. Most of the interviews were conducted in late 2003 and 2004. Database and Internet research was conducted by researchers familiar with the Chinese language, thus including the much richer documentation available in Chinese. Research reports were sent back to the interview partners and feedback was requested to correct erroneous interpretations and, to ensure greater validity of the data. In each case multiple sources of information were used to increase the reliability of observations. Although only representing a small selection of Chinese companies, the collected R&D data were compared to an international database of R&D locations and investment hosted by the Research Center for Global R&D Management at Tsinghua University in Beijing.

3. The significance of Chinese R&D internationalization

Most Chinese companies are relatively young (and therefore comparatively small) and focused on domestic markets. A World Bank survey of 1,500 high-technology companies in China found that they averaged only about 600 employees and were between 10-15 years old. Even well-known Chinese TNCs tend to be small: Lenovo, China's largest personal-computer manufacturer, has a turnover of only 4% of IBM's (at least before its acquisition of IBM's personal computer business in late 2004), and Haier, China's most famous brand (according to a 2003 survey) had sales of $9.7

billion in 2003. Furthermore, 50% of the Chinese firms' supply network is located within their cities, and 75% within China, as Ed Steinfeld (2002) notes in his analysis of the World Bank 2001 report. Much of the spending on R&D seems to be directed towards technological learning (Kim 1997), but little of it results in truly innovative products. Rather than building dominance in a particular industry through technological progress, Chinese companies tend to diversify into other sectors in order to exploit economies of scale. As Steinfeld (2002: 14) notes, Chinese "firms focus on activities with low barriers to entry. Once the cost pressures become too intense, rather than moving upward into higher end activities or taking the time to develop proprietary skills, the firms diversify into other low entry barrier markets. The products themselves ... are standardized." As a result, most of Chinese R&D is opportunistic and hardly standard-setting.

Given these rather sobering interpretations of the quality of Chinese R&D, what is the scale of international R&D by Chinese companies? Unfortunately, no representative data exists, but an effort was made to get an indication of the magnitude of this R&D using data from other developing countries. Earlier research indicated that at least in developed countries, up to 70% of international R&D was conducted by the top-150 global companies. In an attempt to approximate the volume of international R&D conducted, the author took the fifty largest TNCs from developing countries, eliminated non-technology companies (33 remained), summed up their weighted foreign sales (UNCTAD 2001a), and assumed an average of 2% R&D intensity per firm. Given an average lag of approximately 50% of R&D internationalization behind foreign sales (estimated on the basis of von Zedtwitz and Gassmann 2002), this resulted in a total overseas investment in R&D of about $500 million annually for the leading firms from developing countries. This is equivalent to the R&D budget of a single reasonably sized technology-intensive TNC and hence hardly impressive given the scope of this research.

The Chinese firms in the studied sample operated 77 R&D units, 40 in China and a surprisingly high number of 37 abroad (see figure 3). However, most of these R&D units are quite small in size, with a few exceptions such as Huawei's software laboratory in Bangalore (550 engineers in 2003 and expected to grow to more than 2,000 by 2005). Haier alone operated ten small-scale research units abroad, which focused on technology monitoring and other non-indigenous research activities. The 26 R&D units in developed countries were predominantly located in the United States (11) and Europe (11), and mostly serving as listening post or in product design roles. Japan, with only two Chinese R&D units seems to be somewhat under-represented in this sample, probably due to the small sample size. However, even in the complete database of 776 international R&D units, Japan only accounts for 55 or approximately 7% of total foreign R&D laboratories.

Eleven of those 37 foreign R&D units (just under one third) are located in developing countries, thus falling into Type 4 laboratories (figure 4). Chinese firms account for about half of all international R&D sites owned by another developing nation. Some of these R&D units are extremely small (e.g. there are literally just a handful of people in Pakistan and the Islamic Republic of Iran), but India has attracted quite substantial Chinese R&D investment.

Figure 3. International spread of leading Chinese R&D-intensive TNCs, 2004

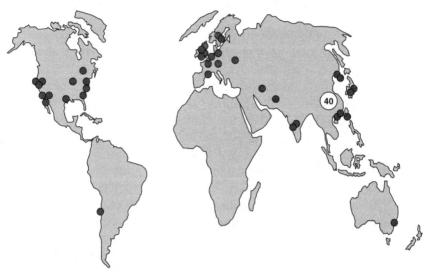

Source: information collected by the author.

Figure 4. International R&D of Chinese TNCs in developed and other developing countries, 2004

	Type 2: Modern	Type 1: Traditional
Advanced Home Country	**0 / 0** All / Intl	**0 / 0** All / Intl
	Type 4: Expansionary	Type 3: Catch-Up
Developing	**51 / 11** All / Intl	**26 / 26** All / Intl
	Developing	Advanced

Host
Country

Source: information collected by the author.

To conclude, even if only physical internationalization of Chinese R&D is considered (ignoring, for the moment, funding of research at non-Chinese universities and participation in international research programmes), China's R&D globalization has already reached a level comparable to some smaller but more developed European countries.

3. Determinants of R&D internationalization of Chinese TNCs

a. Motivation and objectives

"Every multinational will set up in China. Margins are low here. If we don't go outside, we cannot survive" (Haier's chief executive officer Ruimin Zhang, quoted in *The Economist* 2004: 72). Haier, with three industrial parks in the United States, Jordan and Pakistan, ten listening posts in Seoul, Sydney, Tokyo, Montreal, Los Angeles, the Silicon Valley, Amsterdam, Vienna, Taiwan Province of China and Hong Kong (China) and design centres in Lyon, Los Angeles, Tokyo and Amsterdam, is well on its course towards R&D internationalization. A recent addition to their R&D network is a design centre in India, opened in late 2004.

What drives Chinese companies to set up R&D overseas? Given the fact that China itself is a huge and still growing market, most market-oriented R&D is likely to be retained and developed at home. Given also that China still receives a great amount of foreign technology (see Jolly 2004 for the results of a survey of the motivations of Sino-Chinese joint ventures), we can hypothesize that Chinese firms internationalize R&D in order to develop alternate channels of technology sourcing from developed countries – hence, mostly home-base augmenting sites in Kuemmerle's (1997) notation. Automobile manufacturer Dongfeng Motors has established four listening posts in the United States, Germany, the United

Kingdom and France for the purpose of being close to major competitors (not markets) and their technological bases.[3]

Efficiency-driven rationales (see Gassmann and von Zedtwitz 1999 for an overview) such as the exploitation of multiple time zones, the critical mass of R&D, and local cost advantages, hardly play a role for Chinese companies abroad. In fact, many foreign companies go to China because of cost advantages. Hence, Chinese R&D abroad tends to be more expensive than at home, and also less likely to be set up in the first place. However, in cases where Chinese firms operate large manufacturing sites abroad, local R&D has been seen to emerge in support of product localization and process innovation (e.g. Haier's R&D site located with its Camden plant in South Carolina, United States).

While input-related rationales are probably the strongest reasons for Chinese R&D internationalization in developed countries, market and output-related determinants may explain the establishment of R&D in other developing countries such as the Islamic Republic of Iran, Jordan and Chile. Haier prides itself for customer sensitivity. For instance, it developed air conditioners to cope with particularly adverse desert conditions in the Middle East, and designed washing machines that could also handle cleaning vegetables in rural Asia. ZTE's R&D sites in Chile and Pakistan are dedicated to local product adaptation, thus supporting local business development. However, the emergence of R&D in other developing countries is still in its infancy.

---

[3] Note that Dongfeng recently reorganized itself to become a major 50% joint venture company with Nissan Motors of Japan. The new Dongfeng-Nissan R&D centre in Guangzhou has an investment of $40 million and serves as a platform to combine Japanese automotive technology with Chinese standards and product requirements.

Political, regulatory and governmental factors were not mentioned as having a strong impact on the decision where to set up international R&D sites. However, as more and more Chinese companies develop indigenous intellectual property, foreign companies and states are attacking Chinese companies abroad over their earlier infringements on intellectual property rights at home. As a result, Chinese companies are barred from entry into foreign markets based technologies that they use domestically. Local R&D centres could overcome these difficulties by developing local technology, which, in the process, would build new technological competencies for Chinese firms abroad.

International R&D is often also a consequence of mergers and acquisitions. Although Chinese companies have been more of a target than a source of mergers and acquisitions, this seems to be changing, as shown by the investments of Shanghai GM in GM Daewoo and the acquisition of Germany's Schneider by TCL. Thus, R&D units of acquired companies become part of the Chinese firm's R&D network, often making international coordination necessary.

b. Evolution of R&D

The past two decades produced a number of descriptions of strategies for internationalization of R&D and innovation. Based on Perlmutter's (1969) and Bartlett and Ghoshal's (1989) model of internationalization of organization, Gassmann and von Zedtwitz (1999) developed an evolutionary model of international R&D organization, which fits our purpose of studying the early stages of international Chinese R&D. They describe five types of international R&D organizations: ethnocentric centralized R&D (with a dominant R&D centre serving far-away markets), geocentric centralized R&D (where the R&D centre engages in cooperative projects with customers and other research institutes), the R&D hub (with the R&D centre serving as the central information and decision-making platform for all global R&D units), polycentric decentralized R&D (of R&D units with little global alignment and coordination) and, the integrated R&D network (in which all R&D units are equal partners and information and decision-making is freely shared).

Companies without international R&D units have either ethno- or geocentric centralized R&D organizations. In the research sample, this is the case for Lenovo, Netease, CNPC and Longshine. Netease, an Internet service company with almost 200 million registered accounts, actually shifted its development centre from San Francisco, California, where it was originally founded, to Beijing and Guangzhou, as the company relocated to China. Most of the technology is imported from the United States, but a large engineering staff writes code and programmes targeted at the Chinese market. Some of its engineers are foreigners who prepare Netease for more global innovation challenges. Other companies have engaged in a number of cooperative projects and alliances, for instance, Lenovo with Intel and Microsoft, and CNPC with Shell and ExxonMobile. They are becoming more open, and hence overcome ethnocentrism for the benefit of a more geocentric outlook.

Moving towards greater physical international R&D presence are companies like Datang, Founder, Kelon and Dongfeng. Datang had some less successful experience of joint ventures with foreign companies such as Lucent of the United States, but have now formed joint ventures with Philips, Samsung, and UTStarcom. It seems on track with R&D internationalization as it explores greater use of its Iranian R&D site. Its chief executive officer has a PhD from a Belgian university and work experience in a Siemens R&D laboratory. Founder recently set up an R&D laboratory in Scotland, which it plans to expand into its new European headquarters. Dongfeng's alliance with Nissan has obvious consequences of internationalization of product development between China and Japan at the least.

Some companies have firmly established global R&D networks, such as ZTE, Huawei, 3NOD, and Haier. ZTE established its first three foreign R&D centres in the United States and Chile in 1998, and has since founded more R&D laboratories in the Republic of Korea and Sweden. Huawei also has solid international R&D experience. It was the first Chinese company to set up an R&D centre in Bangalore in 2000, earmarking over $100 million for the Indian R&D site, which it expects to serve the Indian subcontinent, West Asia and Africa as strategic markets. With 550 engineers in 2003, it was expected to grow to a staff of 2000 by 2005. Eighty-five per cent of the R&D staff are Indian nationals, as the purpose is to tap into the rich Indian expertise in software design, 3G mobile communications, wireless infrastructure, and network management, etc. Huawei also operates joint ventures with Siemens, 3C, Qualcomm and Microsoft to position itself favourably in the upcoming next-generation mobile communication technology. Almost 46% of its employees are in R&D, although due to the lower labour costs in China, the overall R&D to sales ratio of 10% is more in line with industry averages.

c. Barriers and problems

What are some of the greatest barriers and problems of Chinese companies to expand R&D internationally? In part, they are reflected in typical internationalization problems of companies from developing countries, but some are more specific to China, and some are specific to R&D. Chinese companies face three principal challenges in that respect (Steinfeld 2002).
- They have a size disadvantage: due to their inferior size, they cannot compete head on with much larger TNCs.

- They continue to emphasize local business integration despite increasing international sales. For instance, supply chains are still highly local or regional, and there is little integration with global technology suppliers. As a consequence, Chinese companies are often barred from more value-added activities, and focus on low-cost competition, and hence are unable to engage in product differentiation as a source of competitive advantage.

- They also lack sufficient product innovation. Such innovation would be required for higher profit margins, rather than just reducing costs through efficiency innovation. While simple efficiency innovation produces advantages for manufacturing and customers, it also locks in Chinese companies in mostly domestic-oriented innovation.

Additionally, some companies have to deal with a number of drawbacks relating to lack of resources, lack of experience, and entry barriers in new markets.

- *Lack of cash and resource.*: Although China is an expanding market, profit margins are low and therefore only little can be reinvested in R&D. Investment in groundbreaking R&D (as opposed to technology adaptation and product localization) is more costly, and the first movers are likely to experience a loss of market share. Hence, there is less investment in indigenous R&D , which is the lifeblood of global R&D networks.

- *Lack of management expertise.* Chinese companies have little experience in running or just participating in international companies, and so few of them are qualified for international R&D management assignments. Overseas returnees have been invited to take a stronger   lead, but essentially one of the most important phases of corporate internationalization would thus be carried out by outsiders.

There is little efficiency advantage to go elsewhere for R&D as China is already offering a very favourable price-to-performance ratio for R&D and engineering work. Any local R&D work must be paid for with local revenues, which are generated as local start-up businesses and hence are often reinvested in business development rather than long-term product development.

While younger university graduates speak English better, senior and middle R&D staff have no or little command of English, which is the international language of business and technology. It will take several years before more linguistically trained engineers will have entered the rank and file to support R&D internationalization (incidentally, many of Haier's middle managers are quite young, i.e. in the late 20s).

Chinese management also emphasizes personal networks (*guanxi*) to take decisions and get things done. In international settings, where people are far away from centres of decision-making and corporate networks, foreign R&D managers are at a disadvantage to support their causes and risk permanent loss of social power if removed for too long. Recent initiatives, such as Dongfeng's 'web-enabled R&D systems' are expected to alleviate this problem.

d. Strategies of R&D internationalization

Overall, it seems that truly global R&D in Chinese companies is still far away. Current international R&D structures function because of strong personal leadership or because of a military-style command structure. There is little evidence to suggest that foreign R&D networks managed in this manner are sustainable over the long run, but perhaps we are about to witness the creation of a unique Chinese approach to R&D internationalization. Based on the China example, we can make the following propositions.

- Firms from developing countries are more likely to internationalize R&D into developed countries because of their shortage of domestic technologies, and because of various limitations to serve foreign markets technologically.

- Firms of developing countries will internationalize R&D into other developing countries opportunistically, i.e. when following local customer requests. As a consequence, they may reap long-term first-mover advantages in less privileged regions of the world.

- Thus, companies with more developed R&D networks create two superimposed R&D networks: one which is innovation capability enhancing, i.e. developing the R&D network's capabilities to understand and conduct cutting-edge technology development by absorbing know-how from developed countries, and one which is innovation capability exploiting, i.e. passing on technologies and technical know-how which has been absorbed earlier and refined for use in other developing countries.

The innovatory capability enhancing/exploiting concept is related to Kuemmerle's (1997) home-base augmenting/exploiting notation, but differs in two important aspects.

- The unit of analysis is the R&D network and its various coordination mechanisms and interactions, rather than a dyadic knowledge transfer relationship between the overseas R&D unit with its home base.

- The focus is on innovation capability and its context-specific actualization, rather than knowledge and information exchanged between R&D units.

4. Limitations

This paper has presented research that suffers from limitations, which ongoing research is trying to overcome.

1. The data set is limited and biased towards a) Chinese companies and b) IT companies. The population size limitation must be solved by systematically screening all Chinese firms of a consistent criterion (e.g. total sales or

total R&D investment). The focus on Chinese companies offers greater in-depth analysis, but limits the potential for generalizing the findings. Similar research needs to be conducted in other countries of similar levels of economic development. The bias towards IT companies is representative of the greater levels of international R&D involvement of Chinese IT companies.

2. The use of R&D units is not a perfect proxy for real R&D internationalization, as a) the average size of R&D units in China may be different from the average size of R&D units elsewhere, and b) the denotation of R&D in China may differ from international usage. However, data on R&D investments and staff deployment are difficult to obtain systematically.

3. With respect to the 2x2 matrix of the four types of international R&D research, the selection of parent companies for inclusion of R&D sites of their international affiliates must follow globally consistent and reasonable criteria. The current data of international R&D locations has been collected using the top companies of developing countries and benchmarking them against top companies of developed countries. Although the latter group is much larger than the former, it must be ensured that companies are considered for the same reason and up (or rather) down to a certain level of e.g. annual turnover or R&D investment. Research is ongoing to compensate for this shortcoming.

This analysis is thus still preliminary, and the suggested findings must be considered in the light of these weaknesses.

5. Conclusion

In this paper, the argument was made that internationalization of R&D from developing countries is rising. Four types – and phases – of international R&D were discerned. As an example of Type 3 and Type 4 R&D internationalization,

Chinese companies illustrated some of the motivations, strategies, and difficulties that such companies face. More research is required in terms of deepening the understanding of Chinese technology-intensive firms' strategies as well as those companies from other developing countries such as the Republic of Korea and India. While this research is still incomplete and the conceptual development ongoing, this paper attempts to offer a new framework to analyze international R&D management research as well as a new perspective on specific management models of R&D in developing countries.

References

Bartlett CA and Ghoshal S (1989). *Managing Across Borders: The Transnational Solution.* Boston, MA: Harvard Business School Press.

Bell M and Pavitt K (1993). "Technological accumulation and industrial growth: contrasts between developed and developing countries", *Industrial and Corporate Change* 2(2): 157-210.

Chen J (2003). *Global Innovation.* Beijing: Economic Science Press.

Chiesa V (2000). "Global R&D project management and organization: a taxonomy", *The Journal Product Innovation Management* 17: 341-359.

Dunning JH (1988). *Multinationals, Technology and Competitiveness.* London: Irwin Hyman.

Economist (2004). "Haier's purpose", *The Economist*, Story-I.D. 2524347, 18 May: 72

Gassmann O and von Zedtwitz M (1999). "New concepts and trends in international R&D organization", *Research Policy* 28: 231-250.

Gerpott TJ (1995). "Successful integration of R&D functions after acquisitions: an exploratory empirical study", *R&D Management* 25: 161-178.

Jolly D (2004). "Bartering technology for local resources in exogamic Sino-foreign joint ventures", *R&D Management* 34(4): 389-406.

Katz R and Allen T (1982). "Investigating the Not Invented Here (NIH) syndrome: a look at the performance, tenure, and communication patterns of 50 R&D-project groups", *R&D Management* 12(1): 7-19.

Kim L (1980). "Stages of development of industrial technology in a developing country: a model", *Research Policy* 9: 254–277.

_____ (1997). *Imitation to Innovation: The Dynamics of Korea's Technological Learning.* Boston, MA: Harvard Business School Press.

Kuemmerle W (1997). "Building effective R&D capabilities abroad", *Harvard Business Review* March-April: 61-70.

Lall S (1987). *Learning to Industrialize: The Acquisition of Technological Capabilities in India.* London: Macmillan.

_____ (1990). *Building Industrial Competitiveness in Developing Countries.* Paris: OECD.

Lee J, Bae Z and Choi D (1988). "Technology development processes: a model for a developing country with a global perspective", *R&D Management* 18(3): 235-250.

Medcof JW (1997). "A taxonomy of internationally dispersed technology units and its application to management issues", *R&D Management* 27(4): 301-318.

OECD (2002). *OECD Science, Technology and Industry Outlook 2002.* Paris: Organisation for Economic Co-operation and Development.

Perlmutter HV (1969). "The tortuous evolution of the multinational corporation", *Columbia Journal of World Business* 4: 9-18.

Schaaper M (2004). "An emerging knowledge-based economy in China? Indicators from OECD databases". *OECD STI Working Paper* 2004/4.

Steinfeld E (2002). "Chinese enterprise development and the challenge of global integration". Background paper for World Bank Study "Innovative East Asia: The Future of Growth", Massachusetts Institute of Technology, Cambridge, MA. Mimeo.

Sung CS and Hong SK (1999). "Development process of nuclear power industry in a developing country: Korean experience and implications", *Technovation* 19(5): 305-316.

UNCTAD (1999). *World Investment Report 1999: Foreign Direct Investment and the Challenge for Development.* New York and Geneva: United Nations. United Nations publication, Sales No. E.99.II.D.3.

_____ (2001a). *World Investment Report 2001: Promoting Linkages.* New York and Geneva: United Nations. United Nations publication, Sales No. E.01.II.D.12.

_____ (2001b). *Transfer of Technology. UNCTAD Series on Issues in International Investment Agreements. New York and Geneva:* United Nations publication, Sales No. E.01.II.D.33.

Voelker R and Stead R (1999). "New technologies and international location choice for research and development units: evidence from Europe", *Technology Analysis & Strategic Management* 11(2): 199-209.

von Zedtwitz M and Gassmann O (2002). "Market versus technology drive in R&D internationalization: four different patterns of managing research and development", *Research Policy* 31(4): 569-588.

Xie W and White S (2004). "Sequential learning in a Chinese spin-off: the case of Lenovo Group Limited", *R&D Management* 34(4): 407-422.

_____ and Wu G (2003). "Differences between learning processes in small tigers and large dragons", *Research Policy* 32: 1463-1479.

Technological learning, R&D and foreign affiliates in Brazil[1]

Ionara Costa[2]

Brazil has been one of the main developing country destinations of R&D-related FDI. According to a 2004 survey carried out by the Economist Intelligence Unit (EIU), it was in the sixth position among all countries of the world where TNCs are planning to offshore R&D, and in the third position among developing countries. 11% of the respondents mentioned Brazil, compared to 39% mentioning China and 28% India (EIU 2004). These figures give rise to two questions. (1) What makes Brazil an important site for offshoring R&D? and (2) Why is Brazil lagging behind China and India?

In order to throw some light on these questions, this paper presents some aspects of the technological learning of foreign affiliates located in Brazil and their potential to attract corporate R&D in a context of increasing globalization of such activities. It also addresses how government policies in Brazil have dealt with the technological activities of foreign affiliates.

[1] This paper is based on discussions and studies undertaken at the *Observatory of Strategies for Innovation* (FINEP - OEI/DPP, coordinated by João Furtado, USP/Poli); and more recently, in the framework of a research sponsored by FAPESP on the internationalization of R&D and TNC affiliates in Brazil (coordinated by Sérgio Queiroz, DPCT/Unicamp). The author is grateful to all researchers of the OEI network and to those working in the FAPESP's project, especially to Sérgio Queiroz, whose comments are always constructive. None of them bear any responsibility for eventual errors in this paper.
[2] The views expressed in this study are those of the author and do not necessarily reflect the views of the United Nations, its Member States, or the Institutions to which the author is affiliated.

The point to be made here is that local policies can push further the level of technological learning by foreign affiliates, taking advantage of the process of globalization of R&D.

Foreign affiliates have a solid and strong presence in Brazilian manufacturing. They are amongst the largest firms in the country in terms of value added, employment, new technologies, exports and other economic indicators. The deep-rooted participation of foreign affiliates in Brazilian economic life is the result of a long history of TNC investment.

In Brazil, three major periods of FDI inflows can be distinguished.

- Mid-1950s to the late-1980s: this period was characterized by a strong presence of foreign affiliates, which were instrumental in the process of import substitution industrialization. In technological terms, some adaptive R&D was carried out resulting in minor adaptations and adjustments necessary to better fit imported technologies to local conditions.
- The 1990s, mainly after 1994, were associated with a broad process of *technological upgrading* and *economic restructuring* in response to a much more competitive environment. Technological developments mainly involved the adoption of modern technologies, both of product and process, and new organizational practices, leading to gains in *productivity* and *economic efficiency*.
- More recently, from the late 1990s onwards, there have been signs that a further stage in terms of technological learning is taking place, as TNCs have increasingly included their Brazilian affiliates in their strategies of R&D globalization.

This paper is organized as follows. The next section discusses the characteristics of the third period (the focus of this chapter), arguing that, in general terms, the main drivers of R&D-related FDI in Brazil include technological capabilities previously accumulated by affiliates, mainly for supporting their productive activities; technological competences of other players in the local system of innovation; and specific technological regimes or sectoral patterns. A subsequent section provides an overview of public policies and their impacts on R&D-related FDI. The last section concludes.

1. Innovation and technological efforts on foreign affiliates

Foreign affiliates are important players not only in the Brazilian productive sector, but also in its system of innovation. In fact, the two dimensions are interlinked. Recent innovation surveys[3] have suggested that foreign affiliates innovate more than domestic firms. For instance, according to a composite index of systematic effort, built up from the data of the "Pesquisa da Atividade Econômica Paulista" on R&D personnel, foreign affiliates were given a score of 20, while domestic firms on average had a score of 6, from a maximum level of 100 (Costa and Queiroz 2002, Costa 2003).[4] This suggests that the technological efforts, particularly R&D, carried out in Brazil are still modest when compared with international levels. Moreover, technological learning and R&D remain at *adaptive levels* (Costa and Queiroz 2002).

---

[3] Mainly Fundação Sistema Estadual de Análise de Dados, "Pesquisa da Atividade Econômica Paulista" PAEP 1996 and PAEP 2001 (www.seade.gov.br/produtos/paeponline) and Instituto Brasileiro de Geografia e Estatística, "Pesquisa Industrial de Inovação Tecnológica", PINTEC 2000 and PINTEC 2003 (www.pintec.ibge.gov.br).

[4] The maximum level for this index is derived from the "international frontier" (the efforts of United States firms). The United States data are available from the National Science Foundation (www.nsf.gov/statistics).

In view of the globalization of R&D by TNCs and the fact that Brazil has been receiving some FDI in R&D, it is important to analyse whether and how such recent processes can prompt technological learning in the country. Can the trend of globalization of R&D open opportunities for Brazil to move beyond adaptive levels?

In order to clarify this point, it is necessary to look inside the innovation process of foreign affiliates, and learn more about the forces behind the growth of R&D. In the Brazilian case, three factors should be emphasized: production capacity and technological capabilities; specific features of technologies and products; and local competences.

a. Production capacity, technological competences and R&D

It can be argued that there is a strong relationship between production capacity, technological capabilities and the potential to attract R&D (Queiroz et al., 2003). The size of the Brazilian market reinforces this argument, as it has been a driving force behind the R&D activities performed by foreign affiliates. Foreign affiliates with large and long established production capacities are in a good position to conduct corporate R&D, as the performance of productive activities has led to the accumulation of technological competences and skills.

Cases of global product mandates or development centres are mostly observed amongst long established affiliates that have accumulated technological capabilities in some product or process technologies. In such cases, knowledge embedded in local R&D teams represents assets TNCs can exploit in order to consolidate their market positions. As observed by Queiroz et al. (2003), the capabilities of local affiliates serve to complement those of parent firms.

The automotive industry brings some emblematic cases of strong association of production with R&D, particularly "D" (Consoni 2004, Consoni and Quadros 2003, Furtado et al. 2003). For decades, the largest affiliates of carmakers based in Brazil – Volkswagen, GM, Fiat and Ford – have built up significant levels of managerial and technical skills and capabilities, embedded in large engineering teams; and technical facilities, like styling and prototype centres, laboratories and proving grounds (Queiroz et al. 2003).

The activities of technological development by car makers in Brazil have been focused both on adaptations to local and regional conditions, and the development of local derivatives from global platforms. This process of market-oriented R&D has come to be known as *tropicalization* (Queiroz et al. 2003).

Some affiliates of car makers have been able to move forward in the development process (Consoni 2004). For instance, the engineering team for product development of General Motors Brazil was engaged in the development of the sub-compact model Celta. More recently General Motors Brazil proposed to its headquarters the concept of a global derivative based on the new Corsa, the Meriva model. General Motors Brazil was in charge of the coordination of all stages and teams of the Meriva project (Consoni and Quadros 2003). A similar example is the Tupi project of Volkswagen Brazil, which consisted of the development of a derivative based on the new Polo platform, the Fox model. The Volkswagen Brazil product engineering team, composed of around 700 engineers, was in charge of this project. Furthermore, it has received both the production and development mandates for an entry-level model for the global market (Queiroz et al. 2003).

Therefore, "(…) there has been a change on the quality, complexity and responsibility of the activities the Brazilian engineering has carried out, about to qualify some of the local affiliates to play a major role on global DP [product development]. The tacit knowledge acquired and incorporated by the Brazilian engineering [team] has been an important differential in this process" (Consoni 2004: xv).

In general, the competencies accumulated by local affiliates allow them to compete with their sister companies based in other countries for assignments of R&D activities. The disputes amongst affiliates around the world for roles in the TNCs' network seem to be a relevant aspect of the process of globalization of R&D. Individual countries' systemic capabilities can play another important part in these situations, helping to define for instance, which affiliate will "win" a new R&D laboratory.

b. Technological capabilities and local systems of innovation

While the automotive industry illustrates the case that technological activities by foreign affiliates have been mainly driven by the level of learning they have reached along with their productive activities, the telecom equipment industry sheds light on another important factor: the systemic capabilities, that is, competencies and skills accumulated by other players in the system of innovation. This is reflected in the number of partnerships with universities and research centres. This observation helps to explain the geographical concentration of telecom equipment suppliers in the region of Campinas, in the State of São Paulo. In this area, during the period of state monopoly, competences in telecom technologies were developed in institutions like the Telebras R&D centre (CPqD), and in the State University of Campinas (Unicamp) (Gomes 2003, Queiroz et al. 2003). Nowadays, Campinas has a sound knowledge base for software development and telecom technologies, and a highly qualified workforce in these areas. In fact, "software development is the most important competitive telecom segment in Brazil (…)" (Queiroz et al. 2003: 13).

In some cases, these competencies were developed by domestic firms, many of which were taken over by TNCs in the 1990s during the privatization process. For instance, Zetax and Batik, both domestic firms with strong development capabilities on small switches, were acquired by Lucent in the late-1990s (Galina 2003). As observed by Galina and Plonski (2002: 12), "[s]ince the headquarters of the company [Lucent] did not have this kind of product [small switches], the Brazilian subsidiary is now the world R&D center of this technology". Therefore, it can be claimed that technological competences in some niches can help local foreign affiliates to take part in the global R&D networks. These niches depend to a large extent on the particularities of technologies and products. For instance, "small switching systems are most used in small towns or neighborhoods and it has good potential, especially in developing countries" (Galina and Plonski 2002: 12).

c. Finding niches: technology, product characteristics and local adaptation

The kind of product and/or the sort of technologies are other important factors that help to explain the room for local performance of R&D activities by foreign affiliates. It is not only the need for adaptation of technologies to local conditions, but also the need for taking into account particularities of the local and regional markets into the process of development, and/or the creation of new products that provide room for local R&D activities.

The automotive and telecom industries are both good examples of this. In the automotive industry the importance of taking into account the preferences of consumers during the various stages of conceptualization and development of a new model has been crucial for market success. It helps to explain why the carmakers changed their strategies in terms of product development, giving more room for local engineering teams. In the telecom equipment industry the fact that there are distinct technical patterns in different locations (like "Code Division Multiple Access"/"Time Division Multiple Access", "Global System for Mobile Communications"), both in fixed and mobile technologies, imply the need for local development (Galina 2003). In some cases, different generations of a technology may also open some opportunity for local affiliates. For instance, Ericsson Brazil assumed the development of the second generation of "Code Division Multiple Access" focused on the regional market, while Ericsson United States (San Diego) could concentrate on the third generation of such technologies (Galina 2003).

The pharmaceutical industry is another interesting example, albeit in the opposite direction. As drugs are basically global products, and the development of new drugs is a time consuming and expensive process, local R&D activities by foreign affiliates are almost non-existing. It is worth mentioning that while pharmaceutical TNCs have had productive activities in Brazil for more than 50 years, the competencies they have accumulated along the productive process seem to have contributed little to local technological development.

As illustrated by the examples above, a clear view of the specificities of each industry and segments within them is required in order to better understand the position of foreign affiliates in the globalization of R&D and their potential for moving further in this process. Likewise, it is helpful to comprehend how government can play an active and strategic role in this process.

2. Host-country policies: some lessons from previous experiences

The fact that foreign affiliates constitute a crucial part of the Brazilian innovation system makes the case for elaborating strategic and active policies in order to target new foreign investments into more complex activities, like R&D, and induce already established foreign affiliates to strengthen and deepen their local technological capabilities. How can local policy influence TNCs in terms of their global R&D strategies? The failure or success of previous local policies help to clarify this question.

Since the period of import substitution, Brazilian policies towards FDI have been mainly focused on production capacity building and modernization. Further technological learning has not been a major concern, as attention is concentrated on the amount of FDI into the country rather than on the kind of TNCs' activities attracted.

However, over the past half decade, the debate on the role that foreign affiliates play in terms of technological development seems to have been taking on a new direction. Both scholars and policy makers have been increasingly interested in how activities with greater potential for higher added value can be developed. TNCs have been considered important agents in this respect for two main reasons: first their potential to export, second their better position to carry out R&D and engineering activities. The underlying argument is that the more foreign affiliates based in Brazil are deeply integrated into global R&D networks the higher the value they add locally. This argument is behind the new industrial, technology and foreign trade policy, named as PITCE, which was launched in March 2004 and focuses on innovation, and technological development and foreign trade (PITCE 2003). [5]

Having focused on R&D performed by foreign affiliates (and then on the process of globalization of those activities), this paper now turns to related issues, in order to find out to what extent they helped (or not) to define the technological activities carried out by foreign affiliates. Once again, the automotive, telecom equipment and pharmaceutical industries are illustrative cases.

Regarding the auto industry, local policies have supported the productive and technological dynamic. The *Brazilian Automotive Regime* launched in July 1995 played an important part in stimulating product development by local foreign affiliates. However, this policy was not concerned with R&D investment by foreign affiliates. Its focus was mainly on attracting new investments, increasing production capacity, upgrading products and manufacturing processes and, reaching a broader and deeper insertion of Brazil into the global economy (Furtado et al. 2003; Queiroz at al. 2003). Thus, fiscal incentives were given without any conditionality in terms of local technological development.

Differing from the Automotive Regime, the *Information Technology Laws* ("Leis de Informática": Law

---

[5] The interest of policy makers in the process of globalization of R&D has been increasing. For instance, in some of the preliminary seminars (in March 2005) for the Third National Conference on Science, Technology and Innovation held in October 2005, organized by the Ministry of Science and Technology Policy, there were debates on "R&D by TNCs in Brazil" (4th seminar, March 2005), and "Globalization of R&D: opportunities for Brazil" (5th seminar, March 2005). It is worth mentioning that the PITCE is the background for all debates in preliminary seminars and in the conference itself (see http://www.cgee.org.br/cncti3).

8248/1991, Law 8387/1991, Law 10176/2001, Law 10664/2003, and later Law 11077/2004) explicitly emphasize technological development (Queiroz et al., 2003). In order to be eligible for fiscal incentives, firms are required to carry out R&D investments and, establish partnerships with local universities and research centres (Galina 2003; Roselino and Garcia, 2003; Roselino, 2003). Moreover, the *Information Technology Laws* were complemented by a traditional policy on local content for telecom equipments, implemented by BNDES (the National Bank for Economic and Social Development). In order to receive financial support from BNDES, telecom carriers have to buy locally produced equipment (Furtado et al. 2003).

It is worth mentioning that the PITCE appears to reinforce the technological trajectory in the telecom equipment industry, as software and semiconductors are amongst the five industries it targets. In this sense, the new *Information Technology Law* (Law 11077) launched in December 2004 is an important step, since it is explicitly concerned with where technological development takes place; when the development is locally performed, the fiscal incentives are higher.

In the pharmaceutical industry there has been a clear health policy in terms of enlarging the production base of generic drugs. However, no gains can be observed in terms of local development of technology. In spite of a sound local production capacity, pharmaceutical TNCs appear to have no investment plans for more sophisticated activities by their Brazilian affiliates. "After all, generic drugs are practically commodities that do not require a substantial technological effort" (Furtado et al. 2003: 117). It seems that the PITCE is not changing this orientation, as the pharmaceutical industry has been defined as a priority industry having in mind not local technological development but, the health policy and local production of currently imported drugs.

These three examples reinforce the argument made in this chapter that local policies can play a role as far as R&D activities by foreign affiliates are concerned. The challenge is to learn about the innovative profile of different agents within the local system of innovation, perceiving their technological strengths and weaknesses. In the case of foreign affiliates, it is important to understand the forces behind the role they have played in the global R&D networks.

3. Concluding remarks

Relying on three industry cases, this paper has shed some light on the technological dimension of activities conducted by foreign affiliates in Brazil, in order to have a better understanding of the position of the country in the process of globalization of R&D. Three factors are emphasized here: previous accumulation of capabilities within foreign affiliates; competencies within other agents of the local innovation system; and characteristics of technologies and products. It also outlined some characteristics of local policies, and concludes that they have an important part to play in this process.

The position Brazil has occupied in the globalization of R&D by TNCs can be explained in terms of market reasons. Two related dimensions are stressed: first, the importance of the large size of the Brazilian market and second, the level of technological capabilities accumulated by foreign affiliates that can be exploited by their corporations. Both dimensions define a market-oriented feature of the FDI-R&D related flows into Brazil, as illustrated by the automotive industry. R&D facilities are mainly established in order to support productive activities. Cases of stand-alone laboratories are almost non-existent in Brazil.

Moreover, both the telecommunications equipment and the pharmaceutical industries point to how government policies play a role in the process of globalization of R&D. While in the telecom equipment industry government policies have helped to make Brazil an attractive site for offshoring R&D, in the pharmaceutical industry they have been passive. Public policy can be effective in attracting FDI-related R&D-if combined with prior accumulation of capabilities, and/or a good human resource base, good quality universities and research institutes and further local development.

References

Consoni, F. C. (2004). "Da tropicalização ao projeto de veículos: um estudo das competências em desenvolvimento de produção de produtos nas montadoras de automóveis no Brasil". PhD Thesis, Science and Technology Policy, IG/DPCT, UNICAMP, Campinas. Available at: libdigi.unicamp.br/document/list.php?tid=7.

_____ and Quadros R (2003). "Between centralisation and decentralisation of product development competencies: recent trajectory changes in Brazilian subsidiaries of car assemblers". Paper presented at the XI International Colloquium of GERPISA on "Company Actors on the Look out for New Compromises: Developing GERPISA's New Analytical Schema", Paris, 11-13 June.

Costa I (2003). "Empresas multinacionais e capacitação tecnológica na indústria brasileira". Ph.D. thesis, IG-Unicamp, Campinas, available at: libdigi.unicamp.br/document/list.php?tid=7.

_____ and Queiroz S (2002). "Foreign direct investment and technological capabilities in Brazilian industry", *Research Policy* 31: 1431-1443.

EIU (2004). "Scattering the seeds of invention: the globalisation of research and development". London: Economist Intelligence Unit, available at: graphics.eiu.com/files/ad_pdfs/RnD_GLOBILISATION_WHITEPAPER.pdf.

Furtado J, Zanatta M, Costa I, Strachman E and Queiroz S (2003). "FDI and technology policies in Brazil". European Association of Evolutionary Political Economy (EAEPE) Conference, Maastricht, 7-10 November.

Galina SVR (2003). "Desenvolvimento global de produtos: o papel das subsidiárias brasileiras de fornecedores de equipamentos do setor de telecomunicações". PhD Thesis, University of São Paulo, São Paulo.

_____ and Plonski GA (2002). "Global product development in the telecommunication industry: an analysis of the Brazilian subsidiaries involvement". 9th International Product Development Conference – European Institute for Advanced Studies in Management (EIASM). Sophia-Anipolis, France. May 2002. Available at: www.fia.com.br/pgtusp/pesquisas/arq_pronex/sub01/SGalina%20-%209th%20IPDMC.PDF.

Gomes R (2003). "A internacionalização das atividades tecnológicas pelas empresas transnacionais: elementos de organização industrial da economia da inovação". Ph.D. thesis, IE-UNICAMP, Campinas, Available at: libdigi.unicamp.br/document/list.php?tid=7.

PITCE (2003). "Diretrizes de Política Industrial, Tecnológica e de Comércio Exterior". Brasília: Governo do Brasil, available at: www.federativo.bndes.gov.br/bf_bancos/estudos/e0002388.pdf.

Queiroz S, Zanatta M and Andrade C (2003). "Internationalization of MNCs' technological activities: what role for Brazilian subsidiaries?" Paper presented at SPRU Conference in honour of Keith Pavitt, Brighton, 13-15 November, available at: www.sussex.ac.uk/Units/spru/events/KP_Conf_03/documents/Queiroz.pdf.

Roselino, J. E. (2003). "Informática – Software – OEI/DPP Relatório Setorial". Available at: www.finep.gov.br/portaldpp.

_____ and Garcia R (2003). "Considerações sobre a Lei de Informática: uma avaliação de seus resultados como instrumento indutor de desenvolvimento tecnológico e industrial". In: *VII Encontro Nacional de Economia Política*. Florianópolis. Available at: www.sep.org.br.

Globalization of R&D and economic development: policy lessons from Estonia[1]

Marek Tiits, Rainer Kattel and Tarmo Kalvet[2]

Ever since the evolution of Italian city-states during the Renaissance and the Dutch and German cities in the 16th and 17th centuries, the concept and success of a modern economy have been based on geographical borders that make specialization possible, i.e. allow for the creation of economic clusters enhancing welfare. Economic theory has been based upon the principle stated by Adam Smith, according to which there is a positive link between welfare and the size of a market, because a larger market allows for greater specialization and thus also contributes to the increase of productivity and improvement of living standards (Smith [1776] 1991, Young 1928).[3]

Recent advances of ICT and the liberalization of markets and trade have significantly changed the meaning and role of geography and the proximity of markets. The value chains of the global economy are no longer formed in line with geographical or national borders, but more and more within particular industries. At the same time, an increasing number of economic units are being established and positioned in the states and regions where the socio-economic environment is the most suitable for the production system in question. This means that simpler production tasks are transferred to regions with lower labour costs, but still of relatively high productivity, whereas more complex, higher value-added activities remain in

---

[1] This paper is based on Tiits et al. 2005.

[2] The views expressed in this study are those of the authors and do not necessarily reflect the views of the United Nations, its Member States, or the Institutions to which the authors are affiliated.

[3] Most of the early development economics is based on the same assumption; see Nurkse 1953.

countries with higher living standards. The situation has become increasingly complicated for the regions that can offer neither knowledge-based activities nor low relative labour costs.

In this context, both the enhancement of the competitive advantages of indigenous companies and the selection of locations for FDI are based increasingly on particular economic and technological factors. This makes part of the traditional policies and strategies supporting economic development obsolete or, leaves them without the intended impact. Yet it is obvious that a target of public policies should still be to support the modernization of the economy based on a vigorous private sector.[4] No wonder that the European Commission considers the implementation of the Lisbon Strategy[5] as the highest priority of the EU. However, the Lisbon Strategy does not provide the specific list of the individual steps member States should take in order to accomplish quickly the established objectives. Such detailed regulation does not and cannot exist, because the situations of different European countries are different.[6]

---

[4] Ever since David Ricardo ([1817] 1821), the prevailing idea that a company operating in a particular location should first of all commit itself to activities where the existing environment offers some advantages has remained. However, modern economic theories do not consider such advantages spontaneous; instead, the business environment created by the State has the decisive role in the formation of specialization (Romer 1986).

[5] A ten-year strategy of the EU to become the most competitive and dynamic knowledge-based economy in the world capable of sustainable economic growth with more and better jobs and greater social cohesion.

[6] For theoretical foundations, see Rodrigues 2002. See also the website of the European Commission: http://europa.eu.int/comm/lisbon_strategy/index_en.html.

1. EU membership and economic development

Estonia joined the EU in May 2004 and found itself in a new economic policy environment. Going beyond the transposition of the *acquis communitaire*, Estonia's economic convergence will require a development strategy supporting a more dynamic specialization of the country in the common market. In many respects, the macroeconomic situation environment of Estonia is already similar to that of the older 15 countries of the EU. After the forthcoming introduction of the euro, supervision of monetary policy will be transferred to the European Central Bank, while the Stability and Growth Pact of the EU will establish limitations on fiscal policy. The competence of the EU also includes agriculture and foreign trade, including the application of a customs union towards third countries. For the EU as a whole, such a situation leads to an enormous challenge to develop the economic environment in a manner that is simultaneously appropriate for member States at very different stages of development and, for industries with highly different development trajectories and international networks.

What might Estonia's specialization within the EU be in ten years time? The developments of the past decade will by and large determine the technological and industrial structure of the Estonian economy in the next five to ten years. In Estonia, as in the other Baltic States, most growth has been generated through efficiency gains produced by one-off structural adjustments, privatization and the closing down of unprofitable ventures. An analysis of the development of Estonia since mid 1990s demonstrates that the technological structure of manufacturing has not become more knowledge-intensive or complex, rather the other way round (Tiits et al. 2003).[7] Together with some other new EU members, Estonia is

---

[7] Similar developments have been observed across Central and Eastern Europe; see Watkins and Agapitova 2004, Havlik et al. 2002.

competing for FDI projects with China, India, Latin American countries and the Russian Federation (Reinert and Kattel 2004).

Until recently, relocation of certain parts of the relatively labour- and/or resource-intensive production has been one of the main motivations behind decisions to invest in Central and Eastern Europe.[8] In most cases, foreign affiliates have outperformed domestic enterprises both in terms of knowledge intensity and sales (Damijan et al. 2003). Positive spillovers from FDI however have been relatively limited. Looking at the structure of exports and the competitiveness of manufacturing, it appears that while the other Central and Eastern European countries specialize in various medium-technology activities, Estonia has until now exclusively specialized in timber processing (including furniture, print and paper industries),[9] and certain low-value added activities of Northern European IT and electronics firms.

The sustainability of Estonia's specialization on timber – a resource-intensive and relatively low-technology industry – is far from granted. Nor would it be reasonable to return to Soviet-era light industries or mechanical engineering. Instead, Estonia would need to gradually expand its presence in the medium- and high-technology industries of the next generation, i.e. in the value chains of IT, biotechnology and nanotechnology. The development of such new industries would need to be linked to the existing economic structure and specialization of Estonia. Otherwise the contribution of new high-technology industries to the improvement in living

---

[8] Several authors have concluded, that the interest of foreign investors has been more to exploit, and less to develop local resources (Johansen 2000, Männik 2001: 216).

[9] The Estonian timber processing industry is part of the Scandinavian forestry cluster. Over the past 10 years, it has become the most important source of productivity increase in Estonia (Havlik et al. 2002, Stephan 2003).

standards in Estonia would remain only modest, irrespective of the success of individual companies.[10]

In Estonia, the creation of new jobs is directly dependent on the existing knowledge and skills of the labour force and the compatibility of the education and research system with technological developments in the world and in the Estonian economy. This implies that policies aimed at the continuous modernization of industry and the education and research system which, owing to the logic described above, would need to be industry-specific and, at the same time well coordinated. Whilst the establishment of an efficient system of vocational education, advanced training and retraining and the increase of resources for R&D are equally crucial for the creation of new jobs, none of the aforementioned elements is capable alone of inducing the structural changes in society that are needed for a transition to a knowledge-based economy.

2. Main issues

a. Structure of education and science

Whereas the nominal educational level continues to be relatively high, Estonia has relatively limited lifelong learning, i.e. the renewal of people's skills and knowledge in line with the changing needs of society. While the economy has undergone drastic structural changes, the structure of education and science has evolved de-linked from economic changes. The public R&D funding system as it stands today tends to reproduce past activities rather than contributing to the creation of new ones (Nedeva and Georghiou 2003).

---

[10] Such developments can now be observed in the IT and electronics industries of Estonia and Hungary, where foreign affiliates dominate exports, yet their contribution to the value added remaining in the country and, accordingly to the improvement of living standards is more modest (Kalvet 2004).

At the level of general principles, Estonia has in recent years fully embraced the goals of European innovation policy. However, in practice changes have been slower. R&D and innovation policies usually follow a linear approach to the role of knowledge (including scientific research) in socio-economic development, based upon the belief that massive investment in basic research and the resulting technological development would almost automatically lead to the efficient development of the economy. However, that model that once enabled several technological breakthroughs for world powers (Bush 1945) is not necessarily applicable to small or medium-sized market economies facing resource constraints (Freeman 2002, Nature 2004).

In Estonia, notwithstanding the high rate of unemployment that amounts to as much as over 20% among people under 24 years of age, companies have unremittingly pointed out problems of finding suitably qualified labour (Jürgenson et al. 2005). At the same time, as a result of demographic changes, the number of young people graduating in Estonia from secondary and vocational schools will drop from the year 2008. Since demographic challenges are similar practically everywhere in Europe, severe competition can be expected from better qualified immigrants (OECD 2004: 37, Kauhanen and Lyytinen 2003).

When considering an increase in public investment in education and science, Estonia would first of all need to make the strategic choice regarding in which industries it desires to take the lead, in which industries it would be important to participate actively in EU-wide R&D projects and, in which industries Estonia would want to sustain a minimum level of competence. In addition, modernization of the system of (higher) education in a small country with an aging population requires both the immigration of qualified persons and, a willingness to become an exporter of high-level training.

b. Preferential treatment of IT, bio- and material technologies

Although priority to IT,[11] biomedicine[12] and material sciences has been clearly established in the Estonian research and development strategy *Knowledge-based Estonia 2002-2006* (RTI 2001), no R&D programme has been initiated yet in these areas, nor are there in place any R&D or innovation policy measures targeting these industries. Prompt action would be required in the development of human resources and the economic environment of these areas if Estonia would like to maintain or increase its living standards in the long run. For public policy to be effective, the establishment of priorities must be followed by corresponding substantial changes in institutions and financing.

c. Low private-sector investment into R&D

Having drawn on the lessons of successful Finnish policy in the 1990s, *Knowledge-based Estonia 2002-2006* stresses the importance of the practical application of science. However, as the current structure and competitive advantages of the Estonian economy are more similar to those of Finland in the 1970s and not in the 1990s, the policy of contemporary Finland cannot be directly applied in Estonia.[13]

---

[11] In the OECD countries, more than half of the increase in productivity is derived from innovation in IT and its application. The IT revolution has not ended with the extensive spread of personal computers and the Internet. When it comes to the economic effect of ICT, the actual revolution is likely to be only beginning (Perez 2002).

[12] Massive investment in recent years into bio- and nanotechnologies and new energy technologies in the United States, Western Europe, the Republic of Korea, China and many other countries increases the probability that these industries will in the coming decades experience breakthroughs that will radically change the world.

[13] In the 1970s, massive investments were made in forest-related Finnish industries (including pulp and paper), making the country one of the world's technological leaders in that industry.

Due to the structural problems of the labour market, Estonian companies are short of workers with much lower qualifications than required for proper R&D. At the same time, because of the current investment based phase of development of the economy and the small size of the country, R&D *per se* is not the primary source of competitive advantages or motive for Estonian economic development. It is rather the rapid application of various innovative technologies created elsewhere that prompts Estonian development (Kurik et al. 2002).

In the business enterprise, innovation is *almost always* about novel applications of existing technologies, knowledge and skills. As far as economic development is concerned, the issue is not so much the limited investment of the public sector in R&D, but literally the cost of new technologies and knowledge that Estonian companies need to purchase. Here, it is clear that while the market and competition set the limits of risks, it is the role of public policies to lower those risks for a majority of enterprises and, to create an additional stimulus for the renewal of their competitive edges.

Unfortunately the Estonian education, science, technology and innovation policies are relatively weak on assisting structural change in the economy or supporting technology transfer for upgrading traditional industries. In a market economy, it would be still the task of the state to design an institutional environment suitable for balanced socio-economic development. Consequently, for a substantial part of the Estonian private sector, R&D and innovation are just too expensive and risky.

d. Role of FDI in R&D and innovation

In a small country with an open economy the role of FDI is inevitably large. FDI can substantially strengthen the economy through spillovers and transfer of knowledge to existing industries and, more importantly, initiate the creation and development of new high-technology industries. These roles of FDI have been acknowledged only to a certain degree in Estonian public policy. Little attention has been paid to what motivates investors to invest in Estonia, including in R&D. An overall reduction of the tax burden alone would not be enough. Such a policy could even inhibit the increase of knowledge-intensity of the economy (Bhattacharya et al. 2004, Buffet 2003).

Being a small country, Estonia lacks resources for R&D to the extent necessary to ensure the creation of new international corporations and high-technology industries through spin-off business. However, Estonia can learn from the success achieved by Finland, Ireland, Switzerland and Singapore as a result of a purposeful engagement of FDI in the modernization of the economy. Furthermore, investment by the State in the development of human resources and local competitive assets plays a crucial role in attracting the "right type" of FDI.[14]

Countries such as Estonia would need to exercise caution when developing new high-technology industries, since the development of some science-based industries (e.g. bio- or nanotechnology) alone may not have any immediate effect on living standards. Such high-technology industries are not necessarily connected to the rest of the economy, thereby limiting the value-added created in Estonia. In order to preclude such developments, it is very important to ensure the transfer of knowledge and skills into more traditional spheres that dominate the economy.

---

[14] In that broader context, the success of the Finnish firm Nokia could be due more to "luck" than "regularity" (van Beers 2003, van Grunsven and van Egeraat 1999).

e. Design and coordination of public policy

Even though *Knowledge-based Estonia 2002-2006* is an important strategic document, Estonia today mostly lacks a political and administrative mechanism that would ensure the actual transition of the Estonian economy toward greater knowledge intensity. A regular evaluation and coordination of policies in education, employment, research and development and innovation is almost non-existent. Therefore, practically no one has an overview of the impacts, weaknesses or strengths of the existing policies. As a result, public policy is not sufficiently balanced and lacks a specific goal as regards the improvement of competitiveness (Estonian State Audit Office 2003 and 2004). The connexion between public policies and the problems of the real economy is rather weak. Estonia lacks policy measures that would enable the State to deal with the factors inhibiting the growth of productivity of companies in the timber, electronics, chemical or engineering industries, i.e. industries that currently dominate the economy and exports or, to specifically contribute to the creation of new high-technology industries.

Although policy coordination is a task of the Government and the Prime Minister, policy-making suffers to a large extent from the lack of an interim level of administration that would coordinate the implementation of general horizontal strategies (like *education, research and development, and employment*). This has resulted in conflicting approaches between different sectoral activities. Very few long-term priorities have been set for education, research and innovation policies. However, it is obvious that the more general the public policy measures, the less they are effective.

There would be a need to redesign the system of public policy-making so as to ensure the coordination of policies aimed at a longer-term perspective and the regular analysis of the impacts of such policies. The elaboration of National

Development Plans for the application of the EU Structural Funds could give an impetus to general policy coordination. Yet more needs to be done to achieve better synergies between education, R&D and innovation policies.

In summary, in order to facilitate Estonia's development, a cluster-based strategy for the enhancement of competitiveness would be needed. That strategy could be based upon strategic road maps for particular technologies and economic clusters, while taking into account possible developments both in new high-technology industries and, in the traditionally significant industries (e.g. energy, agriculture etc.). The definition and implementation of such a strategy could only happen through cooperation between scientists, companies and policy-makers aiming at the enhancement of the competitiveness of a particular cluster through the application of essential technological developments (Porter 1990, OECD 2001).

3. Policy recommendations

a. Technology programmes for the enhancement of the competitiveness of economic clusters

In principle, the public sector of Estonia would need to resolve the question of how to ensure that the private sector's problems are properly taken into account in the design and evaluation of policies. A system needs to be established whereby the State can receive feedback on the actual development of the private sector and technology on a continuous basis. To that end, a system of consistent monitoring of industries needs to be created. The establishment of such a system could be one of the key components of a future development strategy. Such a system of design and coordination of policies could highlight as priorities for the five or six economic clusters that are most essential for the technological and socio-economic development of Estonia (e.g. the timber and forestry cluster or, the IT and electronics cluster etc. which in terms of value chains, in the aggregate cover the bulk of the economy).[15]

In practice this means the establishment of permanent working groups of the private and public sectors, the tasks of which would include the production of regular overviews of the possible future developments, current problems and alternative solutions thereof in specific industries. These working groups would need to participate in the coordination, design and evaluation of industrial, educational, science and innovation policies. In the current institutional structure of Estonia, such working groups could logically operate within the field of administration of the Prime Minister and the Research and Development Council.[16]

The primary practical output of the working groups could consist of the development and subsequent evaluation and continuous modernization of the technology programmes that are essential for the development of the clusters in question. The programmes to be created could range from new curricula to schemes aiming at involving foreign affiliates and their parent companies, thus creating:

- new industries where Estonia possesses strong R&D potential in the EU context;
- R&D activities that are connected with real economic activities;
- R&D activities that are interdisciplinary; and

---

[15] As a final outcome, it would be logical to launch national R&D programmes in the fields of administration and by way of cooperation between relevant ministries so as to support the implementation of the relevant industry-level development strategies.

[16] Since the Estonian economy has been rather closely integrated with the Baltic Sea region, that system should also engage the foreign affiliates of TNCs from other Baltic and Northern European countries operating in Estonia.

- R&D activities that are based on cooperation between local and, if necessary, foreign centres of excellence.

b. Horizontal measures

In addition to the commissioning of cluster programmes, Estonia could concentrate on the following four lines of action:

- attracting talented people to work in Estonia and creating an attractive environment for them;
- supporting the transfer of knowledge and technology from foreign affiliates to domestic manufacturing and service industries;
- supporting TNCs and their local affiliates in the fields of R&D and innovation, including reciprocal opening of R&D programmes in the Baltic Sea region and beyond;
- enhancing the capability of companies to apply knowledge created abroad and the capability of scientific research establishments to create new (exportable) knowledge, including training and advanced training; basic research necessary for being current with global scientific and technological developments and, ensuring the required level of the education system.

4. Conclusion

Globalization provides ample opportunities for a more efficient international division of labour, thus contributing to a rise in living standards. The benefits of opening up markets depends on the policy measures implemented in individual countries in response to the strong pressures created by globalization to change existing specializations. There is a role for the State to play in creating positive externalities that would allow domestic enterprises move gradually to more knowledge-intensive, higher value-added activities. Labour, education and innovation policies, focused on some key technologies and supported by industrial policies, can potentially allow for structural changes in the economy, increase innovative capacities of the industry and, finally raise living standards.

References

van Beers C (2003). "The role of foreign direct investment on small countries' competitive and technological position". Government Institute of Economic Research, Helsinki. Mimeo.

Bhattacharya A, Bradtke T, Hemerling J, Lebreton J, Mosquet X, Rupf I, Sirkin HL and Young D (2004). "Capturing global advantage". Boston Consulting Group, Boston, MA. Mimeo.

Buffet W (2003). "Dividend voodoo", *The Washington Post* 20 May: A 19. http://www.washingtonpost.com/ac2/wp-dyn/A13113-2003May19?language=printer.

Bush V (1945). *Science The Endless Frontier. A Report to the President by Vannevar Bush, Director of the Office of Scientific Research and Development, July 1945*. Washington, D.C.: United States Government Printing Office.

Damijan JP, Knell M, Majcen B and Rojec M (2003). "Technology transfer through FDI in top-10 transition countries: How important are direct effects, horizontal and vertical spillovers?" *Working Paper* 17, Institute of Economic Research, Ljubljana.

Estonian State Audit Office (2003). "The activity of the state in channelling funds for supporting entrepreneurship". *Audit Report No. 2-5/03/95*, Estonian State Audit Office, Tallinn. Mimeo.

Estonian State Audit Office (2004). "Results of product development projects supported by Enterprise Estonia". *Audit Report No. 2-5/04/109*, Estonian State Audit Office, Tallinn. Mimeo.

Freeman C (2002). "Continental, national and sub-national innovation systems – complementarity and economic growth", *Research Policy* 31: 191-211.

van Grunsven L and van Egeraat C (1999). "Achievements of the industrial 'high-road' and clustering strategies in Singapore and their relevance to European peripheral economies", *European Planning Studies* 7(2): 145-173.

Havlik P, Landesmann M, Römisch R, Stehrer R and Gillsäter B (2002). "Competitiveness of industry in CEE candidate countries". Composite Paper, European Commission DG Enterprise, Brussels.

Johansen H (2000). "Nordic investments in the former Soviet Baltic frontier: a survey of firms and selected case studies", *Geografiska Annaler, Human Geography* 82(4): 207-219.

Jürgenson A, Kalvet T, Kattel R, (2005). *Business Support Measures in the Budget Strategy for 2007-2013*, Policy Analysis No 9, Tallinn: PRAXIS Center for Policy Studies, available at www.praxis.ee/innopubl/.

Kalvet T (2004). "The Estonian ICT manufacturing and software industry: current state and future outlook". Seville: Institute for Prospective Technological Studies–Directorate General Joint Research Centre, European Commission. *Technical Report* EUR 21193 EN, available at: http://www.jrc.es/home/publications/publication.cfm?pub=1200.

Kauhanen AL and Lyytinen J (2003). "Best before 01 01 2015. Future Makers - Finland 2015: Finnish Success Factors and Challenges for the Future". Final report on the Finland 2015 programme 7. Helsinki: Finnish National Fund for Research and Development.

Kurik S, Lumiste R, Terk E and Heinlo A (2002). "Innovation in Estonian enterprises 1998-2000". *Innovation Studies* 2/2002, Foundation Enterprise Estonia, Tallinn.

Männik K (2001). "The role of foreign direct investments in technology transfer to Estonia". In Varblane U, ed., *Foreign Direct Investments in Estonian Economy*. Tartu: Tartu University Press.

Nature (2004). "Enlightened enlargement", *Nature* 428 (6986) (29 April): 877.

Nedeva M and Georghiou L (2003). "Assessment of the Estonian research development technology and innovation funding system". PREST, The Victoria University of Manchester, available at http://www.riigikantselei.ee/failid/PRESTreport.doc.

Nurkse R (1953). *Problems of Capital Formation in Underdeveloped Countries*. Oxford and New York: Oxford University Press.

OECD (2001). *Innovative Clusters: Drivers of National Innovation Systems*. Paris: Organisation for Economic Co-operation and Development.

_____ (2004). *OECD Science and Innovation Policy: Key Challenges and Opportunities*. Paris: Organisation for Economic Co-operation and Development.

Perez C (2002). *Technological Revolutions and Financial Capital: The Dynamics of Bubbles and Golden Ages*. Cheltenham and Northampton, MA: Edward Elgar.

Porter ME (1990). *The Competitive Advantage of Nations*. London: Macmillan.

Ricardo D ([1817] 1821). *The Principles of Political Economy and Taxation*. London: John Murray.

Reinert ES and Kattel R (2004). "The qualitative shift in European integration: towards permanent wage pressures and a 'Latin Americanisation' of Europe?" *PRAXIS Working Paper* 17, available at: http://www.praxis.ee/data/WP_17_20043.pdf.

Rodrigues MJ, ed. (2002). *The New Knowledge Economy in Europe: A Strategy for International Competitiveness and Social Cohesion*. Cheltenham and Northampton, MA: Edward Elgar.

Romer PM (1986). "Increasing returns and long-run growth", *Journal of Political Economy* 94: 1002-1037.

RTI (2001). *Knowledge-based Estonia: Estonian Research and Development Strategy 2002–2006*. Tallinn: Ministry of Education and Research.

Smith A ([1776] 1991). *The Wealth of Nations, vols. I, VIII*. London: Campbell.

Stephan J (2003). "Evolving structural patterns in the enlarging European division of labour: sectoral and branch specialisation and the potentials for closing the productivity gap". *Sonderheft* 5/2003, Institut für Wirtschaftsforschung, Halle.

Tiits M, Kattel R and Kalvet T (2005). *Made in Estonia: The Wealth of the Nation*. Tartu: Institute of Baltic Studies, available at: http://www.ibs.ee/MiE/.

_____ and Kaarli R (2003). *Competitiveness and Future Outlooks of the Estonian Economy.* Tallinn: State Chancellery.

Watkins A and Agapitova N (2004). "Creating a 21st century national innovation system for a 21st century Latvian economy". *World Bank Policy Research Working Paper* 3457.

Young AA (1928). "Increasing returns and economic progress", *The Economic Journal* 38: 527-542.

PART   III
Policy issues

Linking national science, technology and innovation policies with FDI policies[1]

Thomas Andersson[2]

Much research has been undertaken to settle the controversial issue of whether FDI is good or bad for countries. Most studies concluded that there were positive impacts, because FDI brings efficiency gains, technology and skills transfers, etc. and, because TNCs responsible for FDI generally are unable to internalize all the gains. However, in recent years it has become apparent that the impact of FDI cannot be taken for granted, but critically depends on circumstances. The determinants include policies, TNC strategies, and how the two interact.

Meanwhile, in the wake of globalization, liberalization and technical progress, notably in ICT, the world economy is marked by sweeping structural change.[3] Above all, declining costs of diffusing codified information add to previous reductions in communication and transport costs, and create new tools for firms to divide and specialize operations internationally. At the same time, tacit knowledge remains vital (Pavitt 1998). Firms intensify efforts to upgrade core business, while outsourcing

---

[1] Torbjörn Fredriksson (UNCTAD) has provided valuable comments. A grant from SIDA for research on the knowledge economy is gratefully acknowledged. The author alone is responsible for errors and omissions.

[2] The views expressed in this study are those of the author and do not necessarily reflect the views of the United Nations, its Member States, or the Institutions to which the author is affiliated.

[3] Throughout the developed world, technology- and skill-intensive activities are advancing (OECD 2003). In international trade, the share of high-technology products has increased markedly over the last two decades, although a certain reversal has taken place since 2000 with the consolidation in ICT (UNCTAD 2003).

other functions, and strive to become fully effective in developing, accessing and exploiting – on a global basis – all relevant knowledge in their particular areas of specialization. A key concept is that of innovation (box 1). Dependent on the ability of individuals and firms to discover and implement new ways of doing things, innovation is influenced by a range of capabilities, institutions and policies.

Box 1. The changing nature of innovation

Innovation may be defined as the development of new commercially relevant products or processes. Traditional perspectives have viewed innovation as closely related to science and technology. Mastering the expanding opportunities in scientific and technical progress is becoming an increasingly important source of innovation generating high value-added in developed countries. On the other hand, innovation can take many forms, including the commercialization of science and technology and the development and implementation of new ideas more generally, as in the form of organizational change or inventing new ways of doing things. Innovations that enhance attractiveness and accessibility to customers and users are often essential for commercialization. Furthermore, innovation is the key not only to economic progress, but also to identifying new solutions to pressing social issues, such as an ageing population or environmental degradation. Innovations may be categorized in different ways, including product and process innovations, although there is no clear-cut dividing line between the two.

Innovation must not be conceptualized as a one-dimensional, linear process leading from certain input factors. Innovation is the result of efforts by multiple actors and, is enhanced by their constructive interactions. No single actor generally manages all the skills that are useful, but, complementary competencies are crucial, allowing for a constructive interplay and information exchange between the supply and the demand side in local as well as international markets. Fostering conditions that are favourable to innovation may require reforms in a number of seemingly disparate policy domains.

Source: the author.

The establishment of local R&D generally goes together with a deepened commitment by TNCs to learn about local markets. It may be essential for the generation of knowledge that allows for enhanced efficiency as well as the diffusion of benefits to the host country (Bernstein 1989, Correa 2000). Meanwhile, there are now much enhanced opportunities for investors to establish such facilities in developing economies and countries in transition (UNCTAD 2005). This applies to Central and Eastern Europe and to rapidly developing major industrial strongholds in Asia, such as in China, and in some Latin American countries. Most foreign R&D in developing countries however, remains attracted by a small group of relatively well-off economies, whereas poorer developing countries are neglected. This is particularly worrisome, as official development assistance has diminished in scope, as accessing technologies in other ways is difficult and, as intellectual property rights regimes are fragmented and display deficiencies.

Whereas inter-country flows of technology and skills matter crucially for innovative performance, a country's ability to attract and gain from FDI and foreign R&D will much depend on domestic innovative performance. Any country or region ought to offer conditions that are favourable for the management and exchange of knowledge and technology in ways that support and upgrade their specific assets. Against this backdrop, innovation policy and FDI policy, especially in regard to foreign R&D, hinge together. Yet, the link between them is seldom explored. In this paper, we discuss how these two areas relate to each other, notably in developing countries. The next section reviews the rationale for R&D internationalization and factors influencing technology transfers. In the subsequent section, policy issues in innovation as well as in FDI and foreign R&D are introduced. The interrelated nature of these domains is discussed in the penultimate section. The last section concludes.

1. Organizational changes

For most firms it is becoming untenable to rely on domestic skills and technologies alone. One of the demonstrated benefits of R&D is that it increases the ability of firms to absorb knowledge over great distances (Andersson 1998). TNCs are now faced with significant needs to diffuse and/or absorb technologies worldwide, to an extent that requires a direct presence of R&D facilities in multiple locations. Substantive benefits are derived from the proximity to similar units, favouring clusters and "herd" behaviour in location decisions (von Hippel 1994, Saxenian 1994, Almedia and Kogut 1997). The earlier purpose of primarily adapting products to local markets is now mixed with the motivation to source technology (Sachwald 1998, Mudambi 2002). Firms balance and combine internal capabilities and external uptake for the purpose of innovating more successfully (Cassiman and Veugelers 2002). A tendency towards intensified conflict between home operations and affiliates has also been observed, as reflected in difficulties for TNCs to coordinate global operations (Rajan et al. 2000, Forsgren and Pedersen 2000).

The prevalence of technology and skills transfers in part depends on organizational forms. *Backward linkages* exist when foreign affiliates acquire goods or services from domestic firms, and *forward linkages* when foreign affiliates sell goods or services to domestic firms (both denominated *vertical linkages*). *Horizontal linkages* involve interactions with domestic firms engaged in competing or similar activities.

In most industries backward linkages serve as instruments for spillovers. The drive to raise the quality of inputs serves as an incentive for TNCs to transfer skills to local providers (Chen 1996). Forward linkages are also known to be important, e.g. due to increased competition in supply markets and consumer benefits (Aitken and Harrison 1991, Pack and Saggi 1999). However, in this case the mechanisms for transfers are less well known. Fors (1996) found technology transfers from parents to be strengthened by forward vertical integration, measured as imports of intermediates from the parent company. R&D in affiliates was found not to be decisive, neither for their own productivity nor for other parts of company groups but, a highly significant interactive effect of affiliate R&D and parent R&D on the productivity of affiliates was identified. Given that R&D in affiliates raises the ability to utilize parent technology, foreign R&D would not be expected to substitute for R&D in headquarters. To the extent that the internationalization of R&D is explained by the advancement of intra-firm exports from home countries, it should strengthen knowledge-creation in headquarters. On the other hand, when foreign R&D is driven by horizontal integration, there are fewer prospects for complementarity. Norgren (1995) observed a growing replacement of foreign R&D for home R&D in Swedish TNCs during the 1980s.

As noted, FDI and foreign R&D may also be motivated by options for *technology sourcing*.[4] This is an important reason behind FDI flows between developed countries (van Pottelsberghe de la Potterie and Lichtenberg 2001). There is evidence that sourcing is on the rise as a motive for FDI in developing countries too, and for flows from developing to developed countries. A technical laggard may choose to enter a foreign market through FDI even where that involves substantial costs, because positive spillover effects emanate from locational proximity to a technological leader. (Fosfuri and Motta 1999, Siotis 1999).

---

[4] Various studies conclude that technology sourcing has become an important determinant of the international location of R&D by TNCs (Niosi 1999, Serapio and Dalton 1999, Driffield and Love 2002). According to Narula and Wakelin (2001) for instance, domestic patents were an important long-run determinant of FDI from the United States into Germany, the Netherlands, and Sweden for the period 1973-1993.

Sourcing can occur through the acquisition of firms that possess valuable capabilities or, through the positioning of an affiliate in an environment where participation in local knowledge-generating networks enable uptake. The terms of uptake will depend on the interplay between the TNC on the one hand, and local institutions and market conditions on the other hand. Scientific excellence provides one kind of raw material. Diversity in terms of alternative sources of seed and venture capital funding, and intensive entrepreneurship, account for competition and high prices from the TNC perspective but, is likely to generate more refined input. Technology may further be obtained from other foreign affiliates, meaning that TNCs learn from each other in third countries. This is consistent with the empirical evidence of increasing internationalization of R&D (Cantwell 1995).

In general, TNCs are more prone to network if the local industry is more competitive, that is, if it consists of attractive partner firms. A small technology gap between the foreign affiliate and domestic firms generally facilitates spillovers.[5] A dynamic domestic industry may however, serve as an attraction both for FDI motivated by the exploitation of its own technology and those driven by technology sourcing. If the latter motive dominates, entry through M&A may be anticipated. Conversely, a strong domestic industry and, the prospects for technology diffusion to make it even more productive, may represent a threat to a foreign investor. The greater the dependency of a TNC on its own technology and the greater the potential for technology diffusion, the smaller its tendency to engage in intensive clustering and, the greater its reliance on greenfield investment. If TNCs establish affiliates in enclaves, where neither products nor technologies have much in

---

[5] Girma and Wakelin (2000) define a low gap in terms of a 15% difference in technology intensity, a medium gap as 15-33% and a large gap as more than 33%.

common with those of local firms, spillovers in either direction are likely to be weak.

In either case, local R&D may represent an instrument for TNCs to become more effective in channelling and adjusting technologies and skills for their enhancement locally and/or, in packaging them locally for the sake of generating benefits for the company group as a whole. Strategies to exploit own technology vs. sourcing local technology cannot simply be associated with the benefits or costs for a host country nor for a home country. A dynamic knowledge-intensive region may be anticipated to display extensive knowledge-transfers in both directions. In such an environment, firms and individuals possess high competencies in identifying the most favourable locations and organizational forms for various ventures in research, commercialization and production. Whereas it is generally impossible to make any sharp distinction between the noted functions in practice, various factors may push TNC and affiliate behaviour in one direction or the other. An environment plagued by heavy distortions and a mix of certain strengths but severely lacking capabilities in other respects, is likely to experience one-sided knowledge flows and various undesirable consequences.

Put together, current trends are commonly interpreted as a move from "competence exploitation" to "competence creation" in foreign affiliates or, of a shift from "assembly-type operations" towards "research intensive operations" or "strategic asset-seeking investment". There is the notion of a shift in the orientation of affiliates from "home-base exploiting activity" to "home-base augmenting activity" (Kuemmerle 1996). Furthermore, the geographical reach of affiliates has generally increased significantly. All of these factors in which the internationalization of R&D plays an important role, have consequences for the functioning of affiliates and how they interact with the local environment.

2. Innovation and FDI policy domains

Many countries, developed and developing, now place innovation policy at the very top of their policy agenda, although not always with a clear view of what it entails. The evolution of innovation policy is commonly influenced by its origin, as it has generally emanated from a traditional approach motivated to establish a science base complementary to higher education. Innovation used to be viewed as the linear, one-dimensional output of science and technical progress. However, a number of countries face "paradoxes" in innovative performance, in the sense that R&D is not accompanied by growth. Innovative performance depends on how a range of players interact in bridging the demand for new and better products and, the supply of technology and knowledge. Reduced transaction costs due to the advance of ICT serve to intensify interactions and the innovation process (figure 1).

Figure 1. The intensifying innovation spiral

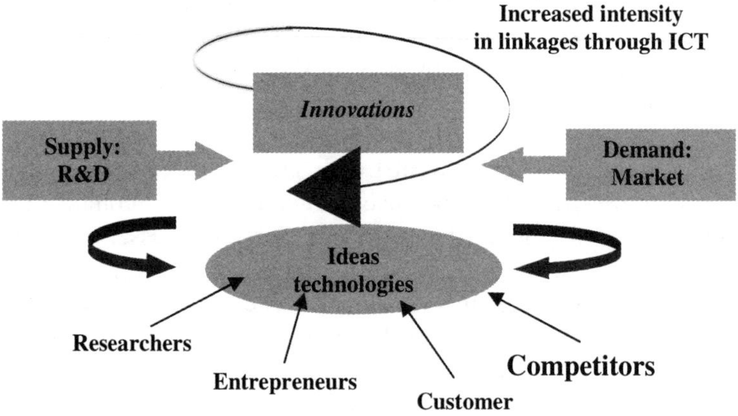

Source: the author.

Innovation depends on a number of related factors. How much R&D is pursued in an economy matters but represents merely one aspect. The composition of R&D is important, as is the access to R&D in the rest of the world. The ability to make use of the results of R&D further depends on knowledge and skills in the work force, on competition, governance, organizational modes, on conditions for entrepreneurship and risk-taking, the quality of public institutions, and so on. Both well-functioning private markets and public service functions are needed, and mismatch between them causes problems (Metcalfe 1995).

It matters greatly whether countries are able to coordinate reforms in ways that can allow firms and individuals to be subjected to consistent incentives and support in regard to their means to innovate. One aspect concerns the degree to which countries pursue governance approaches and evaluations so as to allow for orderly learning processes and thereby, also facilitate gradual improvement. Such learning should not be piecemeal, but allow for gains in efficiency as well as across policy domains and in the division of public-private responsibilities which, on purpose or inadvertently, exert an important influence on conditions for innovation (Andersson et al. 2004). The economies generally viewed as having organized themselves the best in this area include notably Australia, Finland, Singapore and the United Kingdom. Others, such as Chile, China, France, Germany, the Republic of Korea, the Netherlands, Sweden, Switzerland, Taiwan Province of China and the United States, are viewed as strong in individual areas. For all economies however, specific weaknesses or bottlenecks tend to weaken their overall performance. In addition, institutions and policy frameworks are adjusted only slowly, whereas the needs of technology and the economy evolve more quickly.

Traditionally, FDI policies have been based on a reasoning different from that of innovation policies. In order to enhance the local gains of FDI, some governments levied performance requirements on TNCs in the 1960s and 1970s. The effectiveness of such measures was gradually called into question, either because they discouraged FDI in the first place or, because investor behaviour was distorted in unwanted ways. In multilateral negotiations, countries have gradually opted to reduce their room for discretion in levying mandatory requirements on investors, whereas incentives promoting voluntary actions remain viable.

Today, most countries, and also many regions, pursue policies to attract FDI, including particularly high value-added activities. Beyond the measures directly targeting foreign investors, other relevant policies include privatization, regulatory reforms and competition policies, the provision of physical or legal infrastructure, tax incentives, and measures to enhance cooperation between foreign affiliates and local players in order to underpin the establishment of long-term links, the training of local staff, the transfer of skills to domestic firms, and so on. Whereas outright subsidies to foreign investors are (at least publicly) shunned, competitive pressures lead countries into taking various initiatives in order to come out on top in firms' investment decisions, some of which may take the form of a detrimental race for attracting FDI (Oxelheim and Ghauri 2003). However, the complexity of the interplay between foreign and domestic players, with the nature of links and spillover effects dependent on the way in which the strategies of foreign affiliates and local players relate in the specific case, calls for precision rather than generality in FDI-policies. There is a rationale for underpinning the establishment of centres of excellence in priority areas, cherishing specific forums and networks for exchange of information between key domestic and foreign actors and, fostering rather than countering the development of professional networks of business angles and venture capitalists.

3. Interrelated agendas

Countries around the world display markedly varying conditions for innovation. However, they are sharing the experience that no single policy measure or piece of reform is likely to be effective in bringing a radical improvement in innovative capacity. Improving innovative performance may require both enhanced capabilities and revised incentives among a number of actors. On the other hand, specific deficiencies and weaknesses may hamper the overall setup. It is no coincidence that bottlenecks often remain and are difficult to remove over extended periods of time. The prevailing institutional, industrial and social fabric in an economy tends to shape sets of interdependent structures that are not easily overturned. In particular, inefficiencies commonly derive from the influence of well-organized vested interests, which are likely to suffer inevitable losses once their privileges are undercut, whereas the gains are spread relatively thin on the vast number of, often unaware, much less well organized consumers and producers (Olson 1965).

Whereas each country is unique, certain kinds of issues tend to be particularly important in different kinds of countries. There are now examples of impressive leapfrogging processes in the adoption of sophisticated technologies in some LDCs, e.g. through the diffusion of cellular technologies. Even where more basic infrastructure in transport and communication are lacking, LDCs invest disproportionately in ICT and are able to reap significant favourable impacts, if sound regulatory conditions are in place (UNCTAD 2002). However, progress needs to be cherished and recorded differently than in developed countries (Diyamett and Wangse 2001). Developing countries face stern challenges when it comes to raising the capability of private firms to absorb and use the kinds of technology that enter through TNCs.[6] The academic research community and innovative capacity in industry are often de-linked, hampering the establishment of effective incubators and science parks, seed and venture capital funding, etc. At the

---

[6] See Kokko (1994) in the case of Mexico, Kokko et al. (2001) for Uruguay, and Kathuria (2002) and Görg and Strobl (2001) for India.

same time, technology and modern skills need to harmonize with traditional social and community-based conditions that are key to their broad-based application.

In LDCs, innovation is likely to be closely associated with incremental improvement rather than science-based discovery. Here, public support of orderly transactions and the provision of basic education, micro-credit, and also the endorsement of entrepreneurship irrespective of gender and ethnic belonging, are more important for spurring innovation than academic credentials or the protection of intellectual property rights. While managing assets related to the environment and cultural heritage may hold the key to societal gains in local communities (Finger and Schuler 2002), overcoming barriers to learning and new initiatives emanating from traditional perceptions and attitudes may be a prerequisite for adjustment and innovation (Hamel 2005). Capacity building and reform in such respects must precede or match, the attraction and arrival of foreign R&D facilities, if there is to be any wider receptive basis in the form of skilled workers and constructive customers and citizens.

In advanced developing countries, such as Malaysia, Thailand and Brazil, gains from FDI and foreign R&D have been seen to depend on skills upgrading (Best 2001, van Assouw *et al.* 1999). TNC investment in skills is unlikely to suffice unless synergies can be put in place with local training policies and complementary services. On the one hand, inward FDI may account for the decisive impetus for setting off broad-based innovation processes. On the other hand, TNCs cannot be anticipated to induce what is required in a developing country. Whether foreign R&D will be established based on a long-term strategy for knowledge-generation will much depend on the local outlook. Domestic firms, universities and public authorities all count, including in their capacities as prospective partners of relevance to R&D. Some studies have concluded that policy makers should support local competitors in the domestic business community, rather than target FDI (Wang and Blomström 1992).

In order to build appropriate conditions, remove barriers and gain inspiration, international comparison and drawing lessons from other countries can be helpful. Nevertheless, sound innovation policies are not merely legislated from above. Own competencies need to be developed, which is not facilitated by the superficial marketing of the approaches developed by others (Ellerman et al. 2001). Paving the way for innovation requires the involvement of multiple stakeholders or, at least their willingness to accept novel solutions to prevalent problems.

4. Conclusion

Beyond the mere size of FDI and foreign R&D, the question is the roles they play in an economy. Various factors influence observed outcomes. Although most empirical studies conclude that FDI tends to be positive for home as well as host countries, recent work has rendered ambiguous conclusions, and pointed to a complex picture. FDI and globalization bring structural changes that adapt to prevailing conditions and incentive structures.

Today, there is a strong drive for TNCs to diffuse R&D facilities internationally and to allow for enhanced creativity and strategic initiative in individual units. Foreign R&D brings a potential for enhanced commitment to local markets, and adjustment and enhanced diffusion of technology and skills. At the same time, TNCs need to foster an appropriate division of labour between their units for the purpose of internalizing benefits within the group. Individual units are generally motivated to manage knowledge and process or product development in ways that benefit the group as a whole. It is an open question whether they will source technology locally or add technologies so as to help upgrade and strengthen the local environment. Broadly speaking, R&D-facilities in developing countries continue to have limited scope. Given insufficient infrastructure, deficiencies and rigidities in work force skills and labour mobility, weak product/market competition, the absence of local research institutions that can support commercialization of technology in early stages, public authorities and governance that provide risks for technological lock-in and, disconcerting disturbances in playing rules over time, TNCs cannot be expected to establish strongly committed R&D facilities in any particular host country. On the other hand, a country that is not only offering promising growth prospects but, which has put in place an institutional and micro-based fabric conducive to mutually enhancing knowledge exchange, has considerably better chances of enticing foreign technology in ways that will add to the dynamism of the local environment. It is essential that policies in support of FDI and foreign R&D are designed and implemented in tandem with an upgraded broader policy agenda to enhance innovation and growth.

References

Aitken B and Harrison A (1991). "Are there spillovers from foreign direct investment? Evidence from panel data for Venezuela". World Bank, Washington, D.C. Mimeo.

Almedia P and Kogut B (1997). "The exploration of technological diversity and the geographic localization of innovation", *Small Business Economics* 9: 21-31.

Andersson T (1998). "Internationalization of research and development - causes and consequences for a small economy", *Economics of Innovation and New Technology* 7: 71-91.

_____ Schwaag-Serger S, Sörvik J and Wise Hansson E (2004). *The Cluster Policies Whitebook*. Malmö: IKED.

Bernstein J (1989). "The structure of Canadian inter-industry R&D spillovers, and the rates of return to R&D", *Journal of Industrial Economics* 7: 315-328.

Best MH (2001). *The New Competitive Advantage: The Renewal of American Industry.* Oxford: Oxford University Press.

Cantwell J (1995). "The globalisation of technology: what remains of the product cycle model?", *Cambridge Journal of Economics* 19: 155-174.

Cassiman B and Veugelers R (2002). "Complementarity in the innovation strategy: internal R&D, external technology acquisition, and cooperation in R&D. *Social Science Research Network Electronic Paper Collection*, March, www. Papers.ssrn.com/abstract=303562.

Chen E (1996). "Transnational corporations and technology transfer to developing countries". In UNCTAD, ed., *Transnational Corporations and World Development.* London: International Thomson Business Press.

Correa C (2000). "Technology transfer in the WTO agreements". In UNCTAD, ed., *A Positive Agenda for Developing Countries: Issues for Future Trade Negotiations.* New York and Geneva: United Nations, United Nations document UNCTAD/ITCD/TSB/10.

Diyamett B D and Wangwe SM (2001). "Innovation indicators within Sub-Saharan Africa: Usefulness, methodologies and approaches, a specific case for Tanzania". Tanzania Commission for Science and Technology (COSTECH) and Economic and Social Foundation (ESRF), Dar-es-Salaam. mimeo.

Driffield N and Love HL (2002). "Who learns from whom? spillovers, competition effects & technology sourcing by foreign affiliates in the UK". Aston Business School Research Institute, Birmingham, mimeo.

Ellerman D, Denning S and Hanna N (2001). "Active learning and development assistance", *Journal of Knowledge Management* 5(2): 171-179.

Finger M and Schuler P (2002). *Poor People's Knowledge, Promoting Intellectual Property in Developing Countries.* Oxford and New York: Oxford University Press.

Fors G (1996). "R&D and technology transfer by multinational enterprises". Ph.D. dissertation, Stockholm School of Economics, Stockholm.

Forsgren M and Pedersen T (2000). "Subsidiary influence and corporate learning – centres of excellence in Danish foreign-owned firms". In Holm U and Pedersen T, eds., *The Emergence and Impact of MNC Centres of Excellence.* London: Macmillan Press: 68-78.

Fosfuri A and Motta M (1999). "Multinationals without advantages", *Scandinavian Journal of Economics* 101(4), 617-630.

Girma S and K Wakelin (2000). "Are there regional spillovers from FDI in the UK?" *GEP Research Paper* 16, University of Nottingham, Notthingham.

Görg H and Strobl E (2001). "Multinational companies and productivity spillovers: a meta-analysis", *The Economic Journal* 11: F723-F739.

Hamel JL (2005). "Advancing knowledge for meeting MDGs and for sustainable development in Africa: fundamental issues for governance". Draft Working Paper, United Nations Economic Commission for Africa, Addis Ababa, Ethiopia, available at: http://www.uneca.org/estnet/Ecadocuments/Knowledge_for_Susta inable_Development.doc.

Kathuria V (2002). "Liberalisation, FDI and Productivity Spillovers – An analysis of Indian manufacturing firms". Institute of Economic Growth, *Working Paper*, E/220/2002, April, Dehli.

Kokko A (1994). "Technology, market characteristics and spillovers", *Journal of Development Economics* 43: 279-293.

_____, Zejan A and Tansini R (2001). "Trade regimes and spillover effects from FDI: evidence from Uruguay", *Weltwirtschaftliches Archiv* 137(1): 124-149.

Kuemmerle W (1996). "Home base and foreign direct investment in R&D". Ph.D. dissertation, Harvard Business School, Cambridge, MA.

Metcalfe S (1995). "The economic foundations of technology policy: equilibrium and evolutionary perspectives". In Stoneman P, ed., *Handbook of the Economics of Innovation and Technological Change*. Oxford: Blackwell.

Mudambi R (2002). "The location decision of the multinational firm: a survey". In McCann P, ed., *Industrial Location Economics.* Cheltenham: Edward Elgar.

Narula R and Wakelin K (2001). "The pattern of determinants of US foreign direct investment in industrialised countries". In Narula R, ed., *International Trade and Investment in an International World.* New York: Pergamon.

Niosi J (1999). "The internationalization of industrial R&D: from technology transfer to the learning organization", *Research Policy* 28: 107-117.

Norgren L (1995). "Innovative activities in Swedish firms". *Working Paper*, NUTEK, Stockholm.

OECD (2003). *Science, Technology and Industry Scoreboard 2003.* Paris: Organisation for Economic Co-operation and Development.

Olson M (1965). *The Logic of Collective Action.* Cambridge: Harvard University Press.

Oxelheim L and Ghauri P (2003). "The race for investment in the new economy". In Oxelheim L and Ghauri P, eds., *European Union and the Race for Foreign Direct Investment in Europe.* Oxford: Elsevier.

Pack H and Saggi K (1999). "Exporting, externalities and technology transfer". *World Bank Policy Research Working Paper Series* 2065.

Pavitt K (1998). "Technologies, products and organization in the innovating firm: what Adam Smith tells us and Joseph Schumpeter doesn't", *Industrial and Corporate Change* 7(3), 433–452.

Rajan R, Servaes H and Zingales L (2000). "The cost of diversity: the diversification discount and inefficient investment", *Journal of Finance* 55: 35-80.

Sachwald F (1998). "Cooperative agreements and the theory of the firm: focusing on barriers to change", *Journal of Economic Behavior & Organisation* 35: 203-225.

Saxenian A (1994). *Regional Advantage. Culture and Competition in Silicon Valley and Route 128.* Cambridge, MA: Harvard University Press.

Serapio M and Dalton D (1999). "Globalisation and industrial R&D: an examination of foreign direct investment in R&D in the United States", *Research Policy* 28: 303-316.

Siotis G (1999). "Foreign direct investment strategies and firm capabilities", *Journal of Economics and Management Strategy* 8(2): 251-70.

UNCTAD (2002). *E-Commerce and Development Report 2002.* New York and Geneva: United Nations, United Nations document UNCTAD/SDTE/ECB/2.

_____ (2003). *World Investment Report: FDI Policies for Development. National and International Perspectives.* New York and Geneva: United Nations. United Nations publication, Sales No. E.03.II.D.8.

_____ (2005). *World Investment Report 2005: Transnational Corporations and the Internationalization of R&D.* New York and Geneva: United Nations. United Nations publication, Sales No. E.05.II.D.10.

van Assouw R, Carillo J, Mortimore M, Paopongsakorn N and Romjin H (1999). "Industrial restructuring, competitiveness and the role of TNCs: the automobile industry". UNCTAD, Geneva. Mimeo.

van Pottelsberghe de la Potterie B and Lichtenberg F (2001). "Does foreign direct investment transfer technology across borders?", *The Review of Economics and Statistics* 83(3): 490-497.

von Hippel E (1994). "Sticky information and the locus of problem solving: implications for innovation", *Management Science* 40(4): 429-439.

Wang J and Blomström M (1992). "Foreign investment and technology transfer: a simple model", *European Economic Review* 36(1): 137-155.

FDI, R&D and technology transfer in Africa: an overview of policies and practices

John Mugabe[1]

Generally, FDI flows to Africa have expanded only marginally and are still at levels behind those of other developing regions. Africa accounted for less than 1% of global FDI inflows in the late part of the 1990s (UNCTAD 2001). While inflows to developing countries as a group increased from $20 billion to $75 billion between 1981 and 1985, Africa's share of that inflow dropped (UNCTAD 1999). Historically, low rates of FDI inflows to the region have been explained by hostile policies, unstable political environments characterized by civil wars and armed conflicts, a lack of effective regional integration efforts, poor and deteriorating infrastructure, burdensome regulations or, a lack of institutional capacity to implement FDI policies and, a lack of institutional clarity to promote investment in Africa.

There is scant information on the sectoral composition of FDI in Africa. However, available data show that more than 50% of total FDI inflows to the region target natural resource industries, especially mining. The strong relationship between FDI flows and natural resources has been well researched and evidenced. For example, in Ghana investors from the United States, Canada and Australia have been interested in gold. Between 1988 and 1998, more than 60 prospecting and reconnaissance licences were awarded to companies from these countries. In Guinea, more than $130 million had been invested in the Aredor mine by 1996. In the United Republic of Tanzania, mining is the largest industry for FDI and gold is the largest branch. By 1998, total cumulative FDI in mining was

---

[1] The views expressed in this study are those of the author and do not necessarily reflect the views of the United Nations, its Member States, or the Institutions to which the author is affiliated.

estimated at $370 million. Mining attracted 65% of FDI, services 19% and manufacturing 16%. More than 90% of the $1.5-billion FDI inflows to Nigeria in the 1990s targeted the petroleum and natural gas industries. The petroleum industry also dominates FDI in Angola (UNCTAD 2001).

The agricultural industry of the region has attracted more modest FDI. Some of the major projects of the 1990s included Del Monte's investment of more than $9 million in banana plantations in Cameroon, Lonrho's $7.5-million investment in tea estates in the United Republic of Tanzania and, Aberfoyle Holding's multimillion dollar investment in palm oil in Zimbabwe. In the same vein, a large part FDI inflows to Uganda went to the beverages, sugar, and food processing industries and coffee and tea plantations. Uganda also attracted some manufacturing investment in the textiles and packaging industries. Outside manufacturing and agriculture, liberalization of the telecommunication industry attracted considerable investment, while in Ethiopia the hotel industry was the largest recipient (UNCTAD 2001).

African countries are reforming their policies, legislation and institutional arrangements to attract FDI. They treat FDI as a major source of capital for their economic change and development. Some of them are putting emphasis on FDI as a carrier of new scientific knowledge and technological innovation. Investment policies and laws of a growing number of African countries contain provisions aimed at encouraging foreign investors to contribute to the strengthening of the national scientific and technological bases by targeting R&D. Despite these efforts, the R&D content of FDI flows to Africa is very low. This is mainly because of weak domestic R&D capabilities and, in many cases, the absence of institutional mechanisms that provide explicit incentives to investors to target knowledge-based and -intensive activities.

Most African countries have embarked on wide-ranging policy, political and institutional reforms aimed at reducing (and, if possible removing) barriers to entry of foreign capital, particularly FDI. Trade and investment liberalization, privatization and the creation of various incentives for foreign investment have received considerable attention from governments. Regional economic integration bodies and free trade zones have been created to enlarge the size of markets and to adopt common investment regimes at subregional and regional levels. These efforts are based on the recognition that FDI can stimulate economic growth, generate new employment opportunities, promote the transfer of new technologies and contribute to environmental sustainability in the region.

The surge of interest in FDI and TNCs has been so high that in many countries there have been high expectations in terms of what these companies can do, and generally on the development effects of FDI. While FDI can indeed, contribute to national economic and social development in many ways, the engagement and performance of domestic actors are crucial. The effect of FDI largely depends on the policies of the host country. This goes beyond the mere liberalization of economies. Deliberate measures to develop human capital and the physical and social infrastructure can also be valuable ways to enhance the quality of FDI that countries can attract.

The role of TNCs and FDI in promoting the scientific and technological development of African countries is the subject of increasing policy debate and academic research (Oyelaran-Oyeyinka 2004). There is concern about the extent to which FDI stimulates R&D in and transfer of new technologies to Africa. The nature of policies and institutions that are necessary to encourage R&D-based FDI is at the heart of the debate. The main focus of policy makers is on the necessary reforms that should be instituted by their countries to attract the type of FDI that builds or strengthens their domestic R&D capabilities and stimulates local technological learning.

It has been demonstrated in Africa that TNCs tend to invest in R&D in those countries that:

- have a minimum domestic R&D capacity;
- provide legal and economic incentives for knowledge-based investments; and
- provide flexibility for local institutions to forge R&D partnerships with foreign affiliates.

The cases of Kenya and South Africa show that for FDI to contribute to R&D, host-country technology policies should converge with FDI legislation. In the case of Kenya, restrictive measures pertaining to the granting of research permits to foreigners and the absence of a national strategy focusing on knowledge-based investment have restrained FDI to a few R&D-oriented activities, mainly in agriculture. In the case of South Africa, there are explicit strategies to encourage foreign affiliates to engage in R&D. In South Africa local companies and affiliates of TNCs are increasingly investing in R&D. FDI is a growing but not really significant carrier of R&D in the automobile industry, ICTs and agriculture.

References

Oyelaran-Oyeyinka B (2004). "How can Africa benefit from globalization?" *ATPS Special Paper Series* 17. Nairobi: African Technology Policy Studies Network.

UNCTAD (1999). *World Investment Report 1999: Foreign Direct Investment and the Challenge for Development*. New York and Geneva: United Nations. United Nations publication, Sales No. E.99.II.D.3.

_____ (2001). *World Investment Report 2001: Promoting Linkages*. New York and Geneva: United Nations. United Nations publication, Sales No E.01.II.D.12.

PART IV
Comments

FDI and the strengthening of the science and technology capacities in Cameroon

Efa Fouda[1]

Unfortunately, a large part of FDI in African countries such as Cameroon is only linked to the exploitation of primary commodities, notably petroleum extraction and mining. Related to the need for better transforming primary products, it would be desirable to reinforce the R&D and innovatory capacities of these developing countries through attracting FDI in R&D activities. From this perspective, initiatives such as the New Partnership for Africa's Development (NEPAD) should be encouraged. Regarding R&D, national NEPAD programmes, and measures aiming to encourage the establishment of R&D units of the TNCs of developed countries should be put in place. Countries need to reinforce their national science and technological infrastructures (through the creation of science and technology parks, universities and research centres), their programmes to develop human resources and, the implementation of incentive schemes encouraging businesses, including foreign affiliates, to invest in R&D.

To operationalize this vision, the Government of Cameroon has for some time implemented, through the Ministry of Scientific Research and Innovation, a policy aimed at developing scientific knowledge and its application. The final goal is to elaborate sustainable solutions to the socio-economic and cultural problems of Cameroon. The main strategic axes of this policy are:

- the strengthening of scientific and innovatory capabilities;
- the development of human resources (researchers, engineers, research technicians) able to create the scientific

---

[1] The views expressed are those of the author and do not necessarily reflect the views of the United Nations, its Member States, or the Institutions to which the author is affiliated.

knowledge and innovations necessary for the development of Cameroon;
- the elaboration and implementation of research projects contributing to solving the development problems of Cameroon.

The Ministry of Scientific Research and Innovation of Cameroon also seeks to ensure that the national scientific community is able to compete and to communicate with the best scientific teams worldwide in various domains. This way the national scientific community should be aware of, and benefit from, scientific progress and innovation that Cameroon may need, wherever that knowledge is to be found.

The main actors of R&D in Cameroon are the public R&D and innovation units, the State universities and the international R&D organizations established in Cameroon. The Ministry of Scientific Research and Innovation supervises eight public R&D and innovation organizations, employing 500 researchers together:

- L'Institut de Recherche Agricole pour le Développement (agriculture);
- L'Institut de Recherches Géologiques et Minières (geology and mining);
- L'Institut de Recherches Médicales et d'Etude de Plantes Médicinales (medicine and medicinal plants);
- L'Institut National de Cartographie (cartography);
- La Mission de Promotion des Matériaux Locaux (locally produced raw materials);
- Le Centre National d'Education (education);
- Le Comité National de Développement des Technologies (technological development); and
- L'Agence Nationale de Radioprotection (protection against radiation).

Since the reform of higher education in 1993, Cameroon now has six State universities. In 2003, 71,091 students were registered at these universities (of which about 2,000 were Ph.D. students). There are eight international R&D organizations established in Cameroon. They are carrying out joint projects with local laboratories. Cameroon, through the Ministry of Scientific Research and Innovation, has developed scientific collaboration with, on the one hand, several countries (France, the United States, the United Kingdom, Belgium, etc.) and, on the other hand, international organizations dealing with science and technology, such as the relevant bodies of the EU, the French public science and technology research organization "Institut de Recherches pour le Développement", the World Bank, the International Atomic Energy Agency, the World Intellectual Property Organization, the African Development Bank, the Food and Agriculture Organization and, the United Nations Educational, Scientific and Cultural Organization.

Thanks to this intensive international cooperation, the R&D organizations of Cameroon are integrated in the global networks of R&D, allowing them to strengthen the competences and productivity of their researchers. The majority of these researchers have already worked with colleagues from developed countries within the framework of joint projects. The Ministry for Scientific Research and Innovation should ensure, using a comprehensive system of evaluation, that local researchers are in a position to compete, and also cooperate, with the best scientific teams of the world in various fields, so as to be aware of scientific progress necessary for the development of Cameroon. The implementation of these research programmes has had promising results in areas as varied as agriculture and livestock farming, energy, hydrology, cartography, health and nutrition and, the development of materials and natural resources.

The local R&D expertise developed through these measures could be used in various ways, including in projects carried out for foreign affiliates of TNCs established in Cameroon. Generally speaking, TNCs have not yet established R&D units in Cameroon. Nevertheless, the agricultural industry would offer important opportunities for them. Agriculture is an important part of economic activity in Cameroon and, there are important R&D capacities in that industry, notably the Research Institute for Agricultural Development and the University of Dschang. The Research Institute for Agricultural Development is one of the Government's main instruments in the implementation of the national agricultural policy. The Institute carries out a large number of the activities financed by foreign affiliates of foreign TNCs located in Cameroon. The expertise and the innovations provided by the researchers of the Research Institute for Agricultural Development have contributed to the development of an industrial-scale agricultural activity carried out by affiliates of TNCs in the production of bananas, cotton, palm tree oil, cocoa, coffee, maize, rice and beer.

To summarize, the Government of Cameroon is committed to the improvement of the country's attractiveness for FDI in R&D. To that end, concrete measures are being taken to improve the governance of R&D units and to attract investors. Actors operating in the fields of education, R&D and innovation are required to react better to the technological, scientific and professional needs of the private sector and, to contribute to making Cameroon an attractive location for foreign investors looking for human capital.

FDI and R&D: Sri Lanka's experience

Dilip S. Samarasinghe[1]

Many governments have now realized that a key element in achieving economic prosperity, as the developed nations have done in the past, will be to acquire the capability to produce advanced or high value goods. The approach taken by Asian Governments and their investment promotion agencies (IPAs) has been to actively seek FDI, notably in the area now known as business services outsourcing. While India has been the main beneficiary of this trend, other countries, such as Sri Lanka, have also made a few inroads in this direction. One of the main reasons why companies in the developed world opt to set up offices in South Asia is in the competitive relative wages of the sub-continent. Fluency in English is another key consideration. Modern communication systems are another important part. A good example is a United-Kingdom-based medical insurance company that has set up a back office operation in Colombo, Sri Lanka. Every day letters and claims are scanned and sent to Colombo where they are processed. This happens when it is night time in the United Kingdom. By saving on time through back office operations, companies are able to offer a better service to their customers.

FDI in outsourcing has provided benefits to the Asian host countries, including jobs for young people in activities that are new, and indeed never existed before. It is a critical area because it also includes high-technology activities, such as R&D. The jobs created by foreign affiliates of TNCs are also seen as one way to slow down or reverse the massive brain drain from which the sub-region suffers. FDI in advanced areas

---

[1] The views expressed are those of the author and do not necessarily reflect the views of the United Nations, its Member States, or the Institutions to which the author is affiliated.

of research offers new opportunities for the skilled, educated and talented people of South Asia to remain in their countries.

TNCs are technological leaders and their presence in a country will inevitable result in a certain level of technological transfer. They can bring in knowledge on how new goods and services can best be produced. This leads to the enhancement of the skills of labour forces and also brings in more advanced management know-how. It is strategically vital for developing countries and, in particular, those of South Asia to succeed in entering the select club of nations that produce complex or high technology goods and services.

The pursuit of FDI also serves as a basis to channel factors of production in an efficient manner. Countries that have succeeded in attracting FDI have experienced a significant growth and diversification of their exports. In Sri Lanka, companies that come under the purview of the country's IPA produce 60% of export in general and 80% of all industrial exports. In Sri Lanka, FDI based investment represents much of the modern sector of the economy.

A key issue that developing countries need to address is how they interact with TNCs. It is now generally accepted by most developing countries that the presence of TNCs in a country is an indicator of the confidence of a large investor in that country. It is very much like a certificate guaranteeing that the country is politically stable and economically sound. Hence, a country that is able to secure the establishment of TNCs on its territory will be considered, to use a newly coined word, "investment friendly".

In Sri Lanka a central authority, the Board of Investment of Sri Lanka (BOI), handles all FDI. The BOI was founded in 1978 by a government that was seeking to liberalize the country's economy, which had been administered for over two decades under socialistic policies with strong controls and a commitment to import substitution. Sri Lanka was the first South Asian country to move in the direction of economic liberalization before India, Pakistan and Bangladesh.

What makes the BOI different to most IPAs is the sheer scale of its mandate. By the end of 2004, a total of 1,760 companies had invested in Sri Lanka. These employ an estimated 400,000 workers both within and outside the 12 export processing zones. Employees in the zones amount to 121,118. While other IPAs restrict their activities to the attraction of investment, BOI officials call their organization the Investment Management Agency, since it is responsible for attracting investment and processing applications, managing Sri Lanka's export processing zones, managing a separate customs and tax regime aimed at foreign investors and, attracting investment related to infrastructures and other areas. As a result, the organization has a staff of over 1,200 and this size has often led to questions being raised.

While there are many issues confronting FDI in developing countries, the most important consideration a government faces is the type of investment it is seeking to attract. One of the main differences between developing and developed countries is that the developing nations that are seeking to attract FDI are often "generalists". They will not be selective in the type of investment they are seeking to attract, accepting projects from a wide array of sectors and industries.

However, such countries may risk having foreign affiliates whose activity offers very few benefits in economic terms. IPAs of developing nations therefore must move to a more focused approach when seeking investments. Sri Lanka has made some moves in this direction by identifying 12 industries for investment. The BOI has identified those specific priority industries for investment, of which, the eighth is entitled "Research and Development". Unfortunately, there have been very few inflows in the area of R&D despite the incentives offered.

In R&D, to qualify for incentives, a foreign investor needs to invest a minimum of $50,000. If the project is approved by the BOI, and the agreement signed, the government of Sri Lanka will grant the investor a five-year full tax holiday. Thereafter the investor will pay a 15% concessionary tax. The investor will also benefit from import duty exemption on capital goods. However, this will not be granted for raw materials imported and, there is no exemption from exchange controls.

One of the main reasons for the limited amount of R&D-related FDI flows has been the relatively small size of Sri Lanka. Projects that involve higher technology usually require a more technically qualified workforce, which may not always be available in the quantities sought by the TNCs.

Another reason is the relatively limited number of jobs created through R&D. Governments have always been much more keen to attract investment in areas which provide large-scale employment. Employment generation has been also a traditional objective in Sri Lanka. Job creation has been clearly a primary objective of the Government, especially in industries that can employ lower income sections of the community.

Nevertheless, officials of the BOI have also shown interest in high-technology projects, as they help in skill creation, the diversification of the economy and, result in a certain amount of technology transfer.

The success of developing countries in the future will undoubtedly depend on how they succeed in transforming themselves from generalists to specialists and, by that means attract investments that result in greater technological skills. Within the developing world, Sri Lanka has made its first steps towards identifying its priorities, although the results so far are more moderate. It remains to be analysed further why very few inflows in the area of R&D have taken place despite the incentives offered.

Summary of the Expert Meeting on the Impact of FDI on Development, held in Geneva, from 24 to 26 January 2005[1]

1. Introduction

In accordance with its agenda, the Expert Meeting on the Impact of FDI on Development discussed the globalization of research and development (R&D) by transnational corporations (TNCs) and its implications for developing countries. The topic reflected a growing recognition in developing countries of the role played by innovation and R&D in development. Innovation and R&D are essential for upgrading technologies, moving up the development ladder and, catching up with developed countries. In technology generation, transfer and diffusion, developing countries are involving TNCs that are major players in global R&D.

In his opening address, the Chairperson of the Expert Meeting stressed the timeliness of linking the topics of R&D and TNCs. He noted not only that selected developing countries now receive more FDI in R&D, but also that the nature of this FDI is changing, in that it is no longer intended only for local market adaptation. The critical question is whether this phenomenon will spread in the future to a larger number of countries and, if so, under what conditions. (None of this is to deny that there are other key actors in many countries engaged in R&D, namely the public sector and the local private sector). The related practical question is what countries can do to harness the activities of TNCs to their own development objectives. On that point, he asked if R&D is a luxury only to be enjoyed by relatively rich societies, and suggested that its

---

[1] The summary was prepared under the responsibility of the Chairperson of the meeting, H.E. Mr. Enrique Manalo, Ambassador Extraordinary and Plenipotentiary, Permanent Representative of the Philippines to the United Nations Office and other International Organizations in Geneva.

relevance to developing countries in general depends on their aspirations and policies.

Experts discussed the definitions of critical terms in the subject matter. Some stressed the importance of broadening the discussion from R&D to knowledge creation and innovation. Other experts highlighted the importance of looking at cases of R&D in service industries, not just in manufacturing, given that the bulk of world GDP these days is produced by service industries, and R&D is itself a service activity.

2. TNCs and the internationalization of R&D

Several experts stressed that TNCs are only one player in national innovation systems, alongside universities, research centres, domestic firms and other government institutions. TNCs do not generally conduct basic research, and perhaps it is not even desirable to push them into that area. In the interaction of TNCs with other players, the main question is how developing countries can become more actively involved in the process of global knowledge generation and diffusion by leveraging the activities of TNCs in a way that complements domestic efforts.

R&D and innovative activities have generally been confined to the home countries of TNCs much more than manufacturing activities have been. The standard explanation refers to the complexity of R&D activities and the need for geographical proximity. Nevertheless, in recent years R&D activities have become more internationally mobile, and developing countries are starting to become nodes in global innovation networks. In fact, examples of highly complex R&D-related work – such as chip design – were highlighted by some experts to indicate that complexity may no longer constitute a barrier to the internationalization of innovation. It was also noted that the markets for knowledge workers and technology are also becoming increasingly international.

Some experts stressed the importance of distinguishing between different phases in the internationalization of R&D. Until the 1960s, R&D tended to be very "sticky" and stayed in home countries. Starting in the 1960s, the first wave of R&D internationalization involved mainly asset-exploiting R&D aimed at adaptation of products for local markets. The second wave began in the 1970s, and was primarily directed towards adapting specific new products to particular local markets. In the third wave – starting in the 1980s – R&D internationalization was driven by the need for firms to find complementary expertise abroad, notably in other developed countries. This trend was intensified from the 1990s onward and, in the fourth wave there was increasing demand for scientific expertise of a scale and scope that could not be easily met without expanding internationally. In this phase, "asset-augmenting" R&D has also grown in importance.

3. Regional patterns

While most R&D activities remain in developed countries, experts concluded that developing countries are becoming more important as both host and home countries of FDI in R&D. In recent years, China and India have become the leaders of the developing world in FDI in R&D, partly because of their large and fast-growing markets and, their large supply of low-cost engineers and scientists. While noting that important examples of R&D by foreign affiliates could be identified in all parts of the developing world, the experts indicated that these two countries have been particularly successful in attracting "asset-augmenting" R&D conducted with a view to developing processes and products for global markets.

Experts noted that in Latin America and the Caribbean, R&D activities of TNCs are relatively limited, especially when compared to Asia. One of the reasons for this is that in most

Latin American and Caribbean countries, FDI policies focus on attracting large quantities of FDI and do not pay much attention to the nature of FDI. R&D-related FDI in the region is of an adaptive type, with some degree of new product development for local or regional conditions. However, more recently, some countries such as Brazil have begun to attract increasing FDI in R&D oriented towards global applications (for instance in the case of R&D in automobile components).

Experts also observed that Africa attracts low levels of FDI in general and negligible R&D-related activities. The few R&D activities to be found are restricted to the application of existing knowledge rather than the development and application of new ideas. This was attributed to three main reasons: first, the mismatch between science and FDI policies (in many African countries, science, technology and innovation have not been mainstreamed in development strategies); second, a lack of linkages between investment promotion policies and research polices – indeed most FDI policies focus on financial capital rather than knowledge accumulation and human capital (investment promotion agencies (IPAs) for instance, focus more on turnkey projects); and third, the lack of a culture of public-private partnerships. The need to develop proper technology and innovation polices was stressed. In this respect NEPAD was urged to make efforts to improve infrastructure in Africa and enhance the development of science, technology and innovation policies in the region.

4. Drivers and determinants

The issue of the size of host countries was mentioned by various experts as a factor in attracting R&D-related FDI. The situation of the LDCs was singled out since they usually have a very small R&D base. However, it was indicated, that there are areas where R&D-related FDI could develop. In Nepal for example, opportunities exist in the agricultural sector (tea gardening and herbal medicine). It was recognized that LDCs deserve special attention and assistance to help them face the problems they encounter in this area.

A number of drivers of the current internationalization of R&D were identified. One key driver is the increased competitive pressure created by liberalization and technological progress (not least in the area of information and communication technologies), which forces firms to spend more on R&D and speed up the innovation process, while seeking to reduce costs and find the necessary skills. For some developing countries, this has opened new avenues to link up with global innovation networks. Various supply and demand factors, along with policies, were identified as important explanations to why, and in which locations, the globalization of R&D takes place. They include the desire to supply large and fast-growing markets; physical proximity to global manufacturing bases; the search for lower-cost overseas R&D personnel and, for new ideas and innovative capabilities. Dramatic changes in design methodology and organization on the supply side have also contributed to a greater need to globalize R&D work. In India, the existence of reputed national research institutes and, the management style of local companies for example, were also mentioned as specific factors attracting FDI in R&D. The presence of Indian nationals in the R&D centres in developed countries could also influence the choices of TNCs in locating their overseas laboratories in India.

Experts noted that TNCs from developed countries are no longer the only source of R&D-related FDI. There is also growing FDI in R&D (from a low level) by developing country TNCs, e.g. from the Republic of Korea, China and India. Overall, motivations for such FDI tend to be similar to those for R&D-related FDI from developed-country TNCs (for example, to support local sales abroad, to be near global manufacturing bases and, to hire foreign experts). However, while in developing locations the main purpose appears to be to exploit existing knowledge, which is generally second-generation technology, in developed locations the main motivation is to enhance innovative capability by acquiring local knowledge and technology. Some experts concluded that cost advantages are of relatively low importance as a driver for developing-country TNCs' R&D investments abroad. Experts agreed that more research is required on R&D-related FDI from developing countries in order to develop a better understanding of this relatively recent phenomenon.

5. Development impact

A number of positive and negative potential impacts on host economies were identified. Key direct positive impacts mentioned included the creation of well paid employment for scientists and engineers; better use of locally available materials; technology transfer (new equipment, laboratories, etc.); and the design of consumer products better suited to domestic needs. Indirect positive effects include spillovers to local firms; the inculcation of an R&D culture in local firms; the development of new disciplines and specializations at local universities; the development of R&D clusters; and spin-offs of by-products that TNCs do not want to develop themselves.

As for negative impacts of FDI inflows in R&D, experts mentioned the risk of crowding out in the labour market, making it more difficult for local firms to attract talent; the risk of crowding out local research units; limited linkages between foreign affiliates and local firms and institutions and, the risk of domestic R&D activities being closed down as a result of foreign entry, notably through acquisition. The net impact on a host economy depends on the nature of the R&D undertaken and the specific circumstances of the host economy. It was noted that the development of domestic skills and innovation capabilities is essential not only to attract FDI in R&D but also to benefit from such investment.

The extent to which developing countries could benefit from knowledge diffusion and innovation also depends on the extent to which a TNC is embedded in the wider network of research operations, including domestic firms and the public sector. The mode of these interactions is also important, e.g. through non-equity or equity forms; with suppliers, customers, competitors and universities; through outsourcing and offshoring and, through the establishment of research consortia.

6. Policies matter

There was general agreement among experts that active policies by governments could play a leading role in creating and facilitating the right conditions to attract and benefit from FDI in R&D. Key instruments mentioned by experts related to science, innovation and technology policies, as well as FDI policy. Many experts emphasized that in the light of the shift towards more knowledge-based activities and increased internationalization of innovation activities, policy-making aimed at attracting and benefiting from FDI in R&D needs to treat the two policy areas in a holistic and coherent way. Several experts noted that in many countries there is a lack of coherence between FDI policies and science and technology policies.

Among general policy instruments, some experts mentioned FDI liberalization and the strengthening of the national science and technology base, including research institutions. Specific policy instruments that can be considered include incentives, performance requirements, investment targeting, and the provision of public goods (notably low-cost and high-quality infrastructure). One expert noted that in some developing countries, high tariffs on imported R&D-related inputs hamper those countries' efforts to create or develop R&D capabilities. The importance of policies in the area of education and skills development and efforts to strengthen the national innovation system was stressed by various experts. There is also a need to secure an appropriate division of responsibility between central and local governments.

In this context, special attention was paid to the role of IPAs. In many developing countries, IPAs do not pay adequate attention to the potential for attracting FDI that could contribute to knowledge accumulation, but focus rather on capital accumulation in tangible assets. It was argued that an IPA needs to be well embedded in the overall system of national innovation and that promotion activities should be aligned with a country's overall development and innovation strategy. In the case of the Czech Republic, for example, the IPA has a mandate to promote R&D in both foreign and domestic companies; to attract FDI, and to advocate improvements in the country's technological infrastructure; to work with both existing and new investors to encourage new R&D-related investment and, to promote closer linkages between R&D conducted by foreign affiliates on the one hand, and that conducted by domestic firms and universities, on the other.

An important function of policies is to promote closer integration between TNCs and other R&D players, including domestic firms, universities, and other agencies, in order for host countries to capture more of the benefits of knowledge creation and diffusion. Without good linkages between all these actors, knowledge will not be diffused and innovation promoted. Some experts were of the opinion that developing countries in general could benefit from the globalization of R&D but could not use it directly to upgrade the competitiveness of their science and technology capabilities. To do that, they have to complement FDI in R&D with efforts by local public institutions and the private sector. This point was raised for instance, in the case of China and some African countries. A number of experts emphasized the importance of building a balanced partnership between the public and private sectors.

Small developing countries may find it more difficult to successfully engineer strategies to attract FDI in R&D, as they have weak bargaining power and small markets. In this context, a key policy challenge is to set priorities and focus on niches where they could have a comparative or competitive advantage. The development of local capabilities and skills is also essential for such countries to take advantage of opportunities that may be created by the increased mobility of knowledge. Developing such skills and capabilities (particularly in engineering) and building a national strategy to take advantage of opportunities is a long-term process that could take 20 or 30 years, but the rewards of success could be high. Some experts pointed out that it has been done before, showing that small size is not an absolute constraint. Even small developing countries can find a niche for themselves and target specialized R&D activities to match their strengths. A number of experts stressed the need for the prioritization of government goals in related areas. Some argued that regional cooperation could offer opportunities for smaller countries to make themselves more attractive. Others suggested that the building of cooperation and partnership with other countries could go beyond the borders of given regions. International cooperation and the sharing of experience with other countries could also help smaller economies to develop their ability to design and implement appropriate policies.

Experts discussed the role of performance requirements in maximizing the benefits of R&D-related FDI in developing countries. While there was no consensus on the usefulness of performance requirements, several experts noted the importance of distinguishing between mandatory and voluntary performance requirements. The use of mandatory requirements related to R&D and technology transfer is not prohibited by the WTO Agreement on Trade-related Investment Measures, but has become increasingly restricted in various bilateral trade and investment agreements. However, when linked to the provision of incentives (or other advantages), such requirements are still generally permitted. One expert mentioned the importance of offsetting agreements to encourage R&D-related FDI in large infrastructure industries.

Experts also discussed the role of incentives in attracting R&D-related FDI. Some found them useful in attracting investment in R&D in a host country by pioneer firms, who would later be followed by their competitors. Others questioned the usefulness of R&D incentives, arguing that TNCs tend to base their investment decisions in this area more on other factors, such as access to skills. The point was made that countries need to weigh carefully the costs and benefits involved. In this context, some experts noted that benefits to the company receiving an incentive should be assessed against the benefits accruing to the host economy, notably through spillover effects. The R&D work of foreign affiliates has been found in some countries to catalyse domestic R&D activities, help universities to identify new areas where skills development is needed and, attract more interest in technological fields from prospective students.

Several experts raised the issue of intellectual property rights (IPRs). It was noted that high levels of intellectual property protection are often sought by TNCs locating R&D in developing countries but, that the empirical evidence on the impact of IPRs on FDI in R&D is mixed. Referring to the discussion and work undertaken at the WTO in the context of the TRIPS Agreement, one expert recalled that the protection and enforcement of IPRs should contribute to the promotion of technological innovation and to the transfer and dissemination of technology, as stated in Article 7 of the Agreement.

One expert noted that there is a general lack of awareness in developing countries that intellectual property represents assets that can be registered and used to generate income and, that the utilization of intellectual property as assets is important for development in an increasingly knowledge-intensive economy.

Some experts argued that developing countries should develop better intellectual property strategies covering the creation, ownership and commercial leveraging of locally developed research. This would involve, among other things, helping individual researchers and scientists to better understand the importance and value of intellectual property, as well as creating the appropriate incentive structures for them to protect new innovations. It was argued that, by becoming better at using their IPR regimes, developing countries would also become more interesting as partners to TNCs. One expert raised the issue of applying IPR concepts to indigenous knowledge.

Some experts stressed the need to develop public research institutions in the early phases of development. Such initiatives could help to foster the development of skills and raise a country's absorptive capacity. For example, it was noted that Cameroon has established a publicly funded institute for agricultural research around which the Government hopes to create public-private partnerships.

The role of home-country policies in encouraging TNCs to invest in R&D in developing countries and thus bringing benefits to these countries was also addressed. Some experts mentioned the potentially positive role of home countries in promoting FDI in R&D in developing countries, for instance by reducing the risks faced by TNCs when conducting R&D activities in foreign developing countries. The European Union for example, has contributed to the innovation systems of developing countries by encouraging an exchange of scientists and closer interaction between universities in developing countries and EU member countries. On the other hand, an expert noted the concern of some developing countries that developed countries are not fully meeting their transfer of technology obligations in terms of providing incentives to their enterprises to transfer technology to LDCs, as stipulated in the

TRIPS agreement (Article 66.2), although no specific example was given in the course of the discussion on this issue.

7. International cooperation

Some experts called for more bilateral cooperation between relevant institutions in developing and developed countries with a view to fostering policy formulation and stronger innovation systems in the concerned countries. An example of mutually beneficial cooperation between developed home countries of TNCs and developing host countries exists between France and universities in China. This cooperation has resulted in the training of highly qualified researchers who could find employment both in local institutes and firms and in affiliates of French TNCs.

In the light of the importance of innovation and R&D for economic development, and to build on the São Paulo Consensus highlighting the economic development dimension of corporate social responsibility, a suggestion was made to create a list of indicators to assess and measure the contributions of TNCs to the transfer of technology to developing countries. Such a list would be a new contribution to the analysis of the globalization of R&D in the context of assessing what could now be called the "corporate developmental responsibility" of firms.

Some experts regretted that among the Millennium Development Goals of the United Nations, there is no specific goal on science, technology and innovation. The need to explore the possibilities for the international community to support the strengthening of developing countries' national innovation systems, including enhancing opportunities for developing countries to benefit from the internationalization of R&D activities by TNCs, was highlighted. Such support could include both technical and financial assistance.

Contributors

Thomas Andersson is President, Jönköping University, and Professor of International Economics and Industrial Organisation at the Jönköping Business School, Jönköping, Sweden. He is also Chairman of the Board for the International Organization for Knowledge Economy and Enterprise Development (IKED), Malmö, Sweden.

Ionara Costa is Researcher at the United Nations University Institute for New Technologies (UNU-INTECH), Maastricht, the Netherlands.

Dieter Ernst is Senior Fellow at the East West Center, Honolulu, Hawaii, United States.

Efa Fouda is Inspector General, Ministry of Scientific Research and Innovation, Yaoundé, Cameroon.

Tarmo Kalvet is Director of the Innovation Program, PRAXIS Center for Policy Studies, Tallinn, Estonia.

Rainer Kattel is Professor and Chair of Public Administration and European Studies, Tallinn Technical University, Tallinn, Estonia.

John Mugabe is Advisor to the New Partnership for Africa's Development (NEPAD) Science and Technology Forum, Pretoria, South Africa.

Rajneesh Narula is Professor of International Business Regulation at The University of Reading, Reading, United Kingdom.

Robert Pearce is Reader in the Department of Economics at The University of Reading Reading, United Kingdom.

Prasada Reddy is Senior Research Fellow at the Research Policy Institute, Lund University, Lund, Sweden.

Dilip S. Samarasinghe is Director (Media & Publicity) at the Board of Investment of Sri Lanka, Colombo, Sri Lanka.

Marek Tiits is one of the founders of, and Chairman of the Board, of the Institute of Baltic Studies, Tartu, Estonia.

Maximilian von Zedtwitz is Associate Professor at the Research Center for Technological Innovation and the Center for Global R&D Management, School of Economics and Management, Tsinghua University, Beijing, China.

Zhou Yuan is Research Professor and Deputy Director-General at the National Research Center for Science and Technology for Development, Ministry of Science and Technology, Beijing, China.

Selected recent UNCTAD publications on TNCs and FDI
(For more information, please visit www.unctad.org/en/pub)

A. Serial publications

World Investment Reports
(For more information visit www.unctad.org/wir)

World Investment Report 2005. Transnational Corporations and the Internationalization of R&D. Sales No. E.05.II.D.10. $75.
http://www.unctad.org/en/docs//wir2005_en.pdf.

World Investment Report 2005. Transnational Corporations and the Internationalization of R&D. An Overview. 50 p.
http://www.unctad.org/en/docs/wir2005overview_en.pdf.

World Investment Report 2004. The Shift Towards Services. Sales No. E.04.II.D.36. $75. http://www.unctad.org/en/docs//wir2004_en.pdf.

World Investment Report 2004. The Shift Towards Services. An Overview. 62 p.
http://www.unctad.org/en/docs/wir2004overview_en.pdf.

World Investment Report 2003. FDI Policies for Development: National and International Perspectives. Sales No. E.03.II.D.8. $49.
http://www.unctad.org/en/docs//wir2003_en.pdf.

World Investment Report 2003. FDI Polices for Development: National and International Perspectives. An Overview. 66 p.
http://www.unctad.org/en/docs/wir2003overview_en.pdf.

World Investment Report 2002: Transnational Corporations and Export Competitiveness. 352 p. Sales No. E.02.II.D.4. $49.
http://www.unctad.org/en/docs//wir2002_en.pdf.

World Investment Report 2002: Transnational Corporations and Export Competitiveness. An Overview. 66 p.
http://www.unctad.org/en/docs/wir2002overview_en.pdf.

World Investment Report 2001: Promoting Linkages. 356 p. Sales No. E.01.II.D.12 $49.
http://www.unctad.org/wir/contents/wir01content.en.htm.

World Investment Report 2001: Promoting Linkages. An Overview.
67 p. http://www.unctad.org/wir/contents/wir01content.en.htm.

Ten Years of World Investment Reports: The Challenges Ahead.
Proceedings of an UNCTAD special event on future challenges in the area of FDI. UNCTAD/ITE/Misc.45. http://www.unctad.org/wir.

World Investment Report 2000: Cross-border Mergers and Acquisitions and Development.
368 p. Sales No. E.99.II.D.20. $49.
http://www.unctad.org/wir/contents/wir00content.en.htm.

World Investment Report 2000: Cross-border Mergers and Acquisitions and Development. An Overview. 75 p.
http://www.unctad.org/wir/contents/wir00content.en.htm.

World Investment Directories
(For more information visit
http://r0.unctad.org/en/subsites/dite/fdistats_files/WID2.htm)

World Investment Directory 2004: Latin America and the Caribbean. Volume IX. 599 p. Sales No. E.03.II.D.12. $25.

World Investment Directory 2003: Central and Eastern Europe. Vol. VIII. 397 p. Sales No. E.03.II.D.24. $80.

Investment Policy Reviews
(For more information visit
http://www.unctad.org/Templates/Startpage.asp?intItemID=2554)

Investment Policy Review – Algeria. 110 p.
UNCTAD/ITE/IPC/2003/9.

Investment Policy Review – Kenya. 126 p. Sales No. E.05.II.D.21. $25.

Investment Policy Review – Benin. 147 p. Sales No. F.04.II.D.43. $25.

Investment Policy Review – Sri Lanka. 89 p.
UNCTAD/ITE/IPC/2003/8.

Investment Policy Review – Nepal. 89 p. Sales No. E.03.II.D.17. $20.

Investment Policy Review – Lesotho. 105 p. Sales No. E.03.II.D.18. $15/18.

Investment Policy Review – Ghana. 103 p. Sales No. E.02.II.D.20. $20.

Investment Policy Review – Tanzania. 109 p. Sales No. E.02.II.D.6 $20.

Investment Policy Review – Botswana. 107 p. Sales No. E.01.II.D.I. $22.

Investment Policy Review – Ecuador. 136 p. Sales No. E.01.II D.31. $25.

Investment and Innovation Policy Review – Ethiopia. 130 p. UNCTAD/ITE/IPC/Misc.4.

Investment Policy Review – Mauritius. 92 p. Sales No. E.01.II.D.11. $22.

Investment Policy Review – Peru. 109 p. Sales No. E.00.II.D.7. $22.

International Investment Instruments
(Fore more information visit http://www.unctad.org/iia)

International Investment Instruments: A Compendium. Vol. XIV. Sales No. E.05.II.D.8. 326 p. $60.

International Investment Instruments: A Compendium. Vol. XIII. Sales No. E.05.II.D.7. 358 p. $60.

International Investment Instruments: A Compendium. Vol. XII. Sales No. E.04.II.D.10. 364 p. $60.

International Investment Instruments: A Compendium. Vol. XI. 345 p. Sales No. E.04.II.D.9. $60.
http://www.unctad.org/en/docs//dite4volxi_en.pdf.

International Investment Instruments: A Compendium. Vol. X. 353 p. Sales No. E.02.II.D.21. $60.
http://www.unctad.org/en/docs/psdited3v9.en.pdf.

International Investment Instruments: A Compendium. Vol. IX. 353 p. Sales No. E.02.II.D.16. $60.
http://www.unctad.org/en/docs/psdited3v9.en.pdf.

International Investment Instruments: A Compendium. Vol. VIII. 335 p. Sales No. E.02.II.D.15. $60.
http://www.unctad.org/en/docs/psdited3v8.en.pdf.

International Investment Instruments: A Compendium. Vol. VII. 339 p. Sales No. E.02.II.D.14. $60.
http://www.unctad.org/en/docs/psdited3v7.en.pdf.

International Investment Instruments: A Compendium. Vol. VI. 568 p. Sales No. E.01.II.D.34. $60.
http://www.unctad.org/en/docs/ps1dited2v6_p1.en.pdf (part one).

International Investment Instruments: A Compendium. Vol. V. 505 p. Sales No. E.00.II.D.14. $55.

International Investment Instruments: A Compendium. Vol. IV. 319 p. Sales No. E.00.II.D.13. $55.

LDC Investment Guides
(For more information visit
http://www.unctad.org/Templates/Page.asp?intItemID=2705&lang=14)

An Investment Guide to Kenya: Opportunities and Conditions. 92 p. UNCTAD/ITE/IIA/2005/2.

An Investment Guide to Tanzania: Opportunities and Conditions. 82 p. UNCTAD/ITE/IIA/2005/3.

An Investment Guide to the East African Community: Opportunities and Conditions. 109 p. UNCTAD/ITE/IIA2005/4.

An Investment Guide to Mauritania: Opportunities and Conditions. 80 p. UNCTAD/ITE/IIA/2004/4.

Guide de l'investissement au Mali: Opportunités et Conditions. 76 p. UNCTAD/ITE/IIA/2004/1.

An Investment Guide to Cambodia: Opportunities and Conditions. 89 p. UNCTAD/ITE/IIA/2003/6.
http://www.unctad.org/en/docs//iteiia20036_en.pdf.

An Investment Guide to Nepal: Opportunities and Conditions. 97 p. UNCTAD/ITE/IIA/2003/2.
http://www.unctad.org/en/docs/iteiia20032_en.pdf.

An Investment Guide to Mozambique: Opportunities and Conditions. 109 p. UNCTAD/ITE/IIA/4.
http://www.unctad.org/en/docs/poiteiiad4.en.pdf.

An Investment Guide to Uganda: Opportunities and Conditions. 89 p. UNCTAD/ITE/IIA/2004/3.

An Investment Guide to Bangladesh: Opportunities and Conditions. 66 p. UNCTAD/ITE/IIT/Misc.29.
http://www.unctad.org/en/docs/poiteiitm29.en.pdf.

An Investment Guide to Ethiopia: Opportunities and Conditions. 90 p. UNCTAD/ITE/IIA/2004/2.

Issues in International Investment Agreements
(Fore more information visit http://www.unctad.org/iia)

South-South Cooperation in Investment Arrangements. 108 p. Sales No. E.05.II.D.26 $15.

The REIO Exception in MFN Treatment Clauses. 92 p. Sales No. E.05.II.D.1. $15.

International Investment Agreements in Services. 119 p. Sales No. E.05.II.D.15. $15.

State Contracts. 84 p. Sales No. E.05.II.D.5. $15.

Competition. 112 p. E.04.II.D.44. $ 15.

Key Terms and Concepts in IIAs: a Glossary. 232 p. Sales No. E.04.II.D.31. $15.

Incentives. 108 p. Sales No. E.04.II.D.6. $15.

Transparency. 118 p. Sales No. E.04.II.D.7. $15.

Dispute Settlement: State-State. 101 p. Sales No. E.03.II.D.6. $15.

Dispute Settlement: Investor-State. 125 p. Sales No. E.03.II.D.5. $15.

Transfer of Technology. 138 p. Sales No. E.01.II.D.33. $18.

Illicit Payments. 108 p. Sales No. E.01.II.D.20. $13.

Home Country Measures. 96 p. Sales No.E.01.II.D.19. $12.

Host Country Operational Measures. 109 p. Sales No E.01.II.D.18. $15.

Social Responsibility. 91 p. Sales No. E.01.II.D.4. $15.

Environment. 105 p. Sales No. E.01.II.D.3. $15.

Transfer of Funds. 68 p. Sales No. E.00.II.D.27. $12.

Employment. 69 p. Sales No. E.00.II.D.15. $12.

Taxation. 111 p. Sales No. E.00.II.D.5. $12.

International Investment Agreements: Flexibility for Development. 185 p. Sales No. E.00.II.D.6. $12.

Taking of Property. 83 p. Sales No. E.00.II.D.4. $12.

ASIT Advisory Studies (Formerly Current Studies, Series B)

No. 17. *The World of Investment Promotion at a Glance: A survey of investment promotion practices*. UNCTAD/ITE/IPC/3.

No. 16. *Tax Incentives and Foreign Direct Investment: A Global Survey*. 180 p. Sales No. E.01.II.D.5. $23. Summary available from http://www.unctad.org/asit/resumé.htm.

C. Individual Studies

Prospects for Foreign Direct Investment and the Strategies of Transnational Corporations, 2005-2008. 74 p. Sales No. E.05.II.D.32. $18.

World Economic Situation and Prospects 2005. 136 p. Sales No. E. 05.II.C.2. $15. (Joint publication with the United Nations Department of Economic and Social Affairs.)

Foreign Direct Investment and Performance Requirements: New Evidence from Selected Countries. 318 p. Sales No. E.03.II.D.32. $35.http://www.unctad.org/en/docs//iteiia20037_en.pdf

FDI in Land-Locked Developing Countries at a Glance. 112 p. UNCTAD/ITE/IIA/2003/5.

FDI in Least Developed Countries at a Glance: 2002. 136 p. UNCTAD/ITE/IIA/6. http://www.unctad.org/en/docs//iteiia6_en.pdf.

The Tradability of Consulting Services. 189 p. UNCTAD/ITE/IPC/Misc.8. http://www.unctad.org/en/docs/poiteipcm8.en.pdf.

Foreign Direct Investment in Africa: Performance and Potential. 89 p. UNCTAD/ITE/IIT/Misc.15. Free of charge. Also available from http://www.unctad.org/en/docs/poiteiitm15.pdf.

TNC-SME Linkages for Development: Issues–Experiences–Best Practices. Proceedings of the Special Round Table on TNCs, SMEs and Development, UNCTAD X, 15 February 2000, Bangkok, Thailand.113 p. UNCTAD/ITE/TEB1. Free of charge.

Measures of the Transnationalization of Economic Activity. 93 p. Sales No. E.01.II.D.2. $20.

The Competitiveness Challenge: Transnational Corporations and Industrial Restructuring in Developing Countries. 283p. Sales No. E.00.II.D.35. $42.

FDI Determinants and TNC Strategies: The Case of Brazil. 195 p. Sales No. E.00.II.D.2. $35. Summary available from http://www.unctad.org/en/pub/psiteiitd14.en.htm.

D. Journals

Transnational Corporations Journal (formerly *The CTC Reporter*). Published three times a year. Annual subscription price: $45; individual issues $20. http://www.unctad.org/en/subsites/dite/1_itncs/1_tncs.htm.

United Nations publications may be obtained from bookstores and distributors throughout the world. Please consult your bookstore or write:

For Africa, Asia and Europe to:

Sales Section
United Nations Office at Geneva
Palais des Nations
CH-1211 Geneva 10
Switzerland
Tel: (41-22) 917-1234
Fax: (41-22) 917-0123
E-mail: unpubli@unog.ch

For Asia and the Pacific, the Caribbean, Latin America and North America to:

Sales Section
Room DC2-0853
United Nations Secretariat
New York, NY 10017
United States
Tel: (1-212) 963-8302 or (800) 253-9646
Fax: (1-212) 963-3489
E-mail: publications@un.org

All prices are quoted in United States dollars.

For further information on the work of the Division on Investment, Technology and Enterprise Development, UNCTAD, please address inquiries to:

United Nations Conference on Trade and Development
Division on Investment, Technology and Enterprise Development
Palais des Nations, Room E-10054
CH-1211 Geneva 10, Switzerland
Telephone: (41-22) 907-5651
Telefax: (41-22) 907-0498
http://www.unctad.org

QUESTIONNAIRE

Globalization of R&D and Developing Countries
Sales No. E.06.II.D.2

In order to improve the quality and relevance of the work of the UNCTAD Division on Investment, Technology and Enterprise Development, it would be useful to receive the views of readers on this publication. It would therefore be greatly appreciated if you could complete the following questionnaire and return it to:

Readership Survey
UNCTAD Division on Investment, Technology and Enterprise Development
United Nations Office in Geneva
Palais des Nations, Room E-9123
CH-1211 Geneva 10, Switzerland
Fax: 41-22-917-0194

1. Name and address of respondent (optional):

   _____

   _____

2. Which of the following best describes your area of work?

Government	☐	Public enterprise	☐
Private enterprise	☐	Academic or research Institution	
International organisation	☐	Media	☐
Not-for-profit organisation	☐	Other (specify) _____	

3. In which country do you work? _____

4. What is your assessment of the contents of this publication?

Excellent	☐	Adequate	☐
Good	☐	Poor	☐

5. How useful is this publication to your work?

   Very useful   ☐   Somewhat useful   ☐   Irrelevant   ☐

6. Please indicate the three things you liked best about this publication:

   _____

   _____

   _____

7. Please indicate the three things you liked least about this publication:

   _____

   _____

   _____

8. If you have read other publications of the UNCTAD Division on Investment, Enterprise Development and Technology, what is your overall assessment of them?

Consistently good	☐	Usually good, but with some exceptions	☐
Generally mediocre	☐	Poor	☐

9. On the average, how useful are those publications to you in your work?

   Very useful ☐   Somewhat useful   ☐   Irrelevant   ☐

10. Are you a regular recipient of Transnational Corporations (formerly The CTC Reporter), UNCTAD-DITE's tri-annual refereed journal?

    Yes   ☐   No   ☐

    If not, please check here if you would like to receive a sample copy sent to the name and address you have given above   ☐

3057851927